HOLY WAR IN ANCIENT ISRAEL

Holy War
in Ancient Israel

GERHARD von RAD

Translated and edited by
Marva J. Dawn

Introduction by
Ben C. Ollenburger

Bibliography by
Judith E. Sanderson

WILLIAM B. EERDMANS PUBLISHING COMPANY
GRAND RAPIDS, MICHIGAN

Translation from the third edition of *Der Heilige Krieg im alten Israel,*
© 1958 Vandenhoeck & Ruprecht, Göttingen

This edition copyright © 1991 by Wm. B. Eerdmans Publishing Co.
255 Jefferson Ave. S.E., Grand Rapids, Mich. 49503

Library of Congress Cataloging-in-Publication Data

Rad, Gerhard von, 1901-1971.
    [Heilige Krieg im alten Israel. English]
    Holy War in ancient Israel / Gerhard von Rad; translated and edited
by Marva J. Dawn and John H. Yoder.
        p.   cm.
    Translation of: Der Heilige Krieg im altern Israel.
    Includes bibliographical references.
    ISBN 0-8028-0528-0
    1. War—Biblical teaching.   2. Bible. O.T.—Theology.   I. Dawn,
Marva J.   II. Yoder, John Howard.   III. Title.
BS1199.W2R3313   1990
296.3′87873′0933—dc20   90-22465
                                                                CIP

Contents

Abbreviations

SAT	Die Schriften des Alten Testaments
SBL	Society of Biblical Literature
SBT	Studies in Biblical Theology
TBT	*The Bible Today*
ThLZ	*Theologische Literaturzeitung*
VT	*Vetus Testamentum*
VTS	Supplements to Vetus Testamentum
WMANT	Wissentschaftliche Monographien zum Alten und Neuen Testament
ZAW	*Zeitschrift für die alttestamentliche Wissenschaft*
ZDPV	*Zeitschrift des deutschen Palästina-Vereins*
ZWT	*Zeitschrift für wissenschaftliche Theologie*

Since von Rad seems to be using standard German translations for his biblical quotations, we have used primarily the Revised Standard Version to render his examples. When another version was closer to his original emphasis in the German, the source of the English quotation is noted. Numbering of verses in biblical citations follows that of the English editions.

Gerhard von Rad's Theory of Holy War

Ben C. Ollenburger

THE OLD TESTAMENT speaks long and often about war, disturbing many readers and intriguing scholars. Gerhard von Rad was not the first to study the stories of war in the Old Testament,[1] but his book on the topic quickly set the standard for all that followed. *Holy War in Ancient Israel,* which here appears in English for the first time, has become a classic. So persuasive was von Rad's presentation upon its appearance that other scholars could simply refer to it as definitive.[2] In the years since, von Rad's study has attracted significant criticism, in details and in its overall conception, but it remains a genuine classic. Contemporary discussions begin with reference to it. As Patrick D. Miller, Jr., says, "Among those works of the last three decades which have been seminal and influential in Old Testament studies, Gerhard von Rad's small monograph *Der Heilige Krieg im alten Israel* occupies a place of first rank."[3] Consequently,

---

1. Contemporary biblical scholarship tends to use "Hebrew Bible" instead of "Old Testament." However, I will use the traditional term in keeping with von Rad's usage.

2. Cf., e.g., Helmer Ringgren, *Israelite Religion* (Philadelphia: Fortress, 1966), 53.

3. *The Divine Warrior in Early Israel.* HSM 5 (Cambridge, Mass.: Harvard University Press, 1973), 2.

1

it is difficult to understand contemporary discussions of warfare in
ancient Israel, its theology and practice, apart from von Rad. Those
contemporary discussions have been in some measure a series of
footnotes to his work.

The persuasiveness of von Rad's little book—just eighty-four
pages in the original—derives in no small part from von Rad's
ability to compress a wealth of detail within a tightly-woven hypothesis, indeed a theory, that seemingly accounts for everything.
He *wrote* persuasively, and he wrote with a remarkably firm and
consistent grasp of his guiding conception, his theory. He did not
use that theory, in this case his theory of holy war, in place of
evidence or to manufacture evidence; but he did use it as a way
to find and to order evidence, to make sense of that unwieldy mass
of material in the Old Testament that speaks of war. Von Rad was
eclectic. He did not draw his theory of holy war wholesale from
anyone else, nor did he simply read it fresh out of the texts. He
drew on everything at hand, including especially his own research
on other topics in Old Testament studies.[4] Somewhat to the con-
sternation of his interpreters, von Rad tended to cover his tracks.
His works refer sparingly to secondary literature, and they seldom
engage other scholars, or previous ones, in conversation. In this
introductory essay I will try to set out von Rad's *Holy War* in
context—in the context of prior study and in the context of his
own work. If it is true that "no one speaks until he has been
understood,"[5] then there is also merit in showing how von Rad's
Holy War has been received in subsequent treatments of its subject.
I will point to those treatments to conclude this introduction.

4. Important pieces of that research are available in a collection of von Rad's
essays, *The Problem of the Hexateuch and Other Essays* (1966; repr. Philadelphia:
Fortress and London: SCM, 1984). A dozen of these essays were published before
or around the time of *Holy War in Ancient Israel.* See also his *Studies in Deuteronomy.* SBT 9 (London: SCM and Chicago: Henry Regnery, 1953), first published
in 1948. James L. Crenshaw's book, *Gerhard von Rad* (Waco: Word, 1978),
provides an introduction to von Rad and a summary of his work.

5. Robert Sokolowski, *The God of Faith and Reason: Foundations of Christian Theology* (Notre Dame: Notre Dame University Press, 1982), 120.

I

That war figured heavily in ancient Israel's memory has never been in doubt; the Old Testament itself permits no other conclusion. But it was Julius Wellhausen who stated most clearly, and starkly, the significance of war to Israel's religion. Wellhausen began with the straightforward observation that Israel's identity was inherently religious: "The foundation upon which, at all periods, Israel's sense of its national unity rested was religious in its character." The specific content of that religious character, Wellhausen says, "was the faith which may be summed up in the formula, Jehovah is the God of Israel, and Israel is the people of Jehovah."[6] But more than that:

> It was most especially in the graver moments of its history that Israel awoke to full consciousness of itself and of Jehovah. Now, at that time and for centuries afterwards, the highwater marks of history were indicated by the wars it recorded. The name "Israel" means "El does battle," and Jehovah was the warrior El, after whom the nation styled itself. The camp was, so to speak, at once the cradle in which the nation was nursed and the smithy in which it was welded into unity; it was also the primitive sanctuary. There Israel was, and there was Jehovah.[7]

For Wellhausen, then, war was not just a feature of Israel's experience, or even of its religion. Ancient Israel as the people of God was a military camp, and its God was a warrior. War was at the heart of Israel's religion and thus of its identity.[8]

6. *Prolegomena to the History of Ancient Israel* (1885; repr. Cleveland: World, 1957), 433. The quotation is taken from Wellhausen's article, "Israel," reprinted from the *Encyclopaedia Britannica* as an appendix to this English edition of the *Prolegomena* (429-548).

7. *Prolegomena*, 434. Von Rad quotes the same comment from Wellhausen's *Israelitische und jüdische Geschichte*, 3rd ed. (Berlin: Georg Reimer, 1897), 26 [see *Holy War*, 51 n. 14]. Cf. also Rudolf Smend, *Yahweh War and Tribal Confederation: Reflections upon Israel's Earliest History* (Nashville: Abingdon, 1970), 26-27.

8. In his *Prolegomena*, Wellhausen notes that "the heroes of Israelite legend

Wellhausen did not pursue these insights into a discussion of warfare in Israel, or of Israel's theology of war. However, his fundamental insight into the religious character of war in Israel was elaborated by Friedrich Schwally. In 1901 Schwally published a book on "Holy War in Ancient Israel" as part of a series devoted to warfare in "semitic antiquity."[9] His was the first systematic study of the topic, and he conceived it as a comparative ethnographic investigation.[10] Schwally agreed with Wellhausen that Israel itself originated in warfare; Exod. 14 and 15 say so explicitly. Schwally then added to this historical observation an anthropological one: in any religion's most primitive stage, every dimension of life is brought into the religious sphere. From this it follows that Israel would bring warfare into the closest relation with Yahweh right from the beginning. Consequently, to talk about Israel's religion is to talk about war, and one cannot talk about war in Israel as other than a religious phenomenon. Schwally carried these observations further by associating warfare in Israel with the religiously central notion of Yahweh as a covenant God. He took this to mean that the covenant God is equivalent to the warrior God, the God who defends the covenant or federation.

Schwally used the German term *Bund,* "covenant," to refer properly to Israel as a federation, and only in a derivative sense to Israel's theological conception of its relation to Yahweh. He claimed that "covenant" referred first to a federation between Israel and Midian and was then expanded to refer to Israel itself—a

---

show so little taste for war, and in this point they seem to be scarcely a true reflection of the character of the Israelites as known from their history" (321). Of these heroes—the patriarchs—he says, "Brave and manly they are not, but they are good fathers of families, a little under the dominion of their wives, who are endowed with more temper" (320).

9. *Der heilige Krieg im alten Israel,* vol. 1 of *Semitische Kriegsaltertümer* (Leipzig: Deiterich, 1901). Schwally's was the only volume published in the series.

10. Von Rad criticizes Schwally's comparative procedure in *Holy War,* 69-70. Cf. also Manfred Weippert, "'Heiliger Krieg' in Israel und Assyrien: Kritische Anmerkungen zu Gerhard von Rads Konzept des 'Heiligen Krieges im alten Israel,'" *ZAW* 84 (1972): 460-493, esp. 465.

covenant or federation of the people. This understanding of covenant as a federation, Schwally said, provided the basis for a theology of covenant in which God was worshipped as a warrior. And this official, corporate worship—the Israelite sacrificial cult—itself constituted the context in which war was conducted. That can only mean that war, as Israel conducted it, was holy war: it was an activity undertaken by Israel as the army of Yahweh in defense of the federation (covenant), over which Yahweh was sovereign. On the basis of this cultic context of war, Schwally concluded that, for ancient Israel, "war is a continuous, highly expanded sacrifice."[11] The cult was not simply an important feature of warfare or a set of rituals attending it; rather, warfare was an important feature of the cult. Holy war was one centrally important way in which Israel worshipped Yahweh; it had not only a cultic context but a cultic character.

Schwally also highlighted a significant difference between some of Israel's holy war narratives and what can be concluded from both comparative material and other Old Testament texts. Israel and every other nation in antiquity claimed that their gods participated in war and were responsible for giving their warriors victory. But only Israel came to understand this claim to mean that it was unnecessary for warriors to fight. However, Schwally did not count this as a difference in fact, attributing it instead to "later Jewish historiography" and its interests in edification. These led to an exaggeration of the importance of faith in Yahweh's assistance and to minimization of human participation. What seems at first glance to be a difference is simply the result of pietistic history-writing.[12]

The most obvious legacy of Schwally's book is the term "holy war" itself. The Old Testament does not use the term, although it does speak of the "wars of Yahweh" (1 Sam. 18:17; 25:28; Num.

11. Schwally, 59.
12. Pp. 27-28. He cites Josh. 6 and Judg. 7 as examples. Cf. Millard C. Lind, *Yahweh Is a Warrior: The Theology of Warfare in Ancient Israel* (Scottdale, Pa.: Herald, 1980), 24.

21:14). Schwally took the term from the Arabic *jihad,* "holy war."
In classical Islam, *jihad* was a technical term referring to wars
undertaken to convert infidels, specifically the Jewish and Christian population of a territory, and to enforce land and poll taxes
on the non-Islamic population.[13] The term appears first in Greek
literature, in Thucydides (*Peloponnesian Wars* i.112) and Aris-
tophanes (*The Birds* v.556—where it is a war against Zeus!).
Whether or not the term is appropriate to the Old Testament, or
to ancient Israel, depends largely on how its referent is conceived.
On Schwally's conception, and on von Rad's, it is probably the
best choice. In any event, thanks to Friedrich Schwally "holy war"
has become part of the scholarly lexicon.[14]

It was not an Old Testament scholar but a renowned sociologist, Max Weber, who took up and expanded on Schwally's study.
He did so in a series of studies published between 1917 and 1919
and collected in his book, *Ancient Judaism.*[15] As did Schwally,
Weber emphasized both the institution of the cult and the notion
of covenant. Yahweh, Israel's God, was the sovereign of the
covenant. This religious conception, and especially the cult that
nourished it, was the basis for social cohesion in Israel. It was the
basis, then, of the Israelite federation—or, as Weber called it, the
confederacy, the *Bund.* Yahweh was Israel's "contractual part-
ner."[16] And as sovereign of the Israelite confederacy, Yahweh was
its defender.

---

13. Peter C. Craigie, *The Problem of War in the Old Testament* (Grand
Rapids: Wm. B. Eerdmans, 1978), 22-26. In Islam, *jihad* can also refer to
"spiritual warfare," and some contemporary Muslims would take this to be its
proper referent.

14. Cf. John Howard Yoder, "To Your Tents, O Israel: The Legacy of Israel's
Experience with Holy War," *Studies in Religion/Sciences religieuses* 18 (1989):
348.

15. (Glencoe, Ill.: Free Press, 1952). Albert de Pury summarizes Weber on
holy war in "La guerre sainte Israélite: Réalité historique ou fiction littéraire?"
Études théologiques et religieuses 56 (1981): 12.

16. Weber, 131. Weber discusses the nature of Israel's God in ch. 5, entitled
"Social Significance of the War God of the Confederacy" (118-146).

The Israelite confederacy itself, according to unambiguous tradition, represented a war confederation under and with Yahweh as the war god of the union, guaranteeing its social order and creator of the material prosperity of the confederates.[17]

This meant, in Weber's understanding, that Yahweh was of preeminently political importance to Israel. That marked a difference between the religion of Israel and other religions, or other religious possibilities, according to which the deity may be related primarily to the individual or to nature. While neither of these dimensions was lacking in Israel's religion, Yahweh's relation to the political sphere was decisive. Of course, war itself is a political event, but given Israel's notion of the covenant, as Weber understood it with Schwally, war as a political event was also a religious and specifically cultic event. Holy war presupposed the "collective liability" of the confederacy for the violation of covenant obligations on the part of any member.[18] And those obligations were seen to derive, of course, directly from the covenant with God. Thus, wars undertaken against members of the confederacy were holy wars. They were political and religious events, in the earliest period, with a specific form of leadership.

Expanding on a suggestion of Schwally's, Weber argued that during the confederacy *(Bund)* Israel's charismatic prophets (e.g., Deborah and Samuel) exercised a particular role as leaders in war. When the monarchy brought about its fundamental social and political transformation, the ecstatic prophets no longer had a role to play: they were "de-militarized."[19] However, they retained their connection to war as "literati"—as "political ideologists."[20] In an underground manner, and critical of the monarchy, the prophets continued to nurture the spirit of the confederacy, and particularly the idea of Yahweh as a warrior on behalf of Israel.

17. P. 81.
18. P. 137. See also below, n. 24.
19. P. 101.
20. P. 112.

> The seers and prophets independent of the king, the popular heirs
> of the military Nebiim [charismatic prophets], now without com-
> missions, hence, hallowed the time when Yahwe himself as war
> leader led the peasant army, when the ass-riding prince did not
> rely on horses and wagons and alliances, but solely on the god
> of the covenant and his help.[21]

They not only looked back to this golden era of the past, they
projected it into the future in a utopian vision. The prophets preserved an ideology that had no practical application under the
bureaucratic monarchy; what they preserved was thus an *alternative* tradition—alternative to and critical of the monarchy's
routinized, bureaucratic conduct of politics and war.[22]

Weber's remarks about Israelite warfare depend on the use of
"holy war" as an abstract concept, a "type." Weber seems to have
thought there were only three pure instances of holy war—the war
of Deborah and Barak in Judg. 5, the war of the tribes against
Benjamin in Judg. 20, and Saul's war against the Ammonites in
1 Sam. 11.[23] The decisive factor in each was the covenant mutually
obligating the members of the confederacy to defend it, and in each
case—on Weber's interpretation—there was a failure of some part
of the confederacy to honor this obligation.[24] Gerhard von Rad offers

---

21. P. 111. Weber claims that, "just as today, in all countries, we find the
highest measure of war thirst among those strata of literati who are farthest from
the trenches and by nature least military" (112).

22. Weber gives such terms as "traditional," "charismatic," and "routinized"
a technical meaning. He discusses them at length in *The Theory of Social and
Economic Organization* (New York: Free Press, 1964), 324-392.

23. *Ancient Judaism*, 44. There Weber says that "these three cases belong to
the type of 'holy war' . . ."

24. Weber interprets the importance of the incident in 1 Sam. 11 to consist
in "Jabesh's negotiations to capitulate." It was at the news of these negotiations
that Saul "was seized by holy fury sent by Yahwe" (*Ancient Judaism*, 98). In Judg.
5 the issue is the failure of some tribes to answer the call to muster, and in Judg.
20, Benjamin's calumny against the confederacy. When von Rad suggests that
Weber regarded only these wars as holy wars because holy war is "a cultic
institution which historically never became fully manifest" (*Holy War*, 69—von
Rad's only mention of Weber), he seems to miss Weber's point entirely. Ironically,

a definition quite different, but his material account of holy war is
sometimes strikingly similar to Weber's, and his reliance on a generalized theory of holy war—virtually as an "ideal type"—carries at
least an echo of Weber's sociological method.[25]

Wellhausen, Schwally, and Weber set the stage for von Rad's
own presentation; nonetheless, there were other treatments of
Israel's conception of war that preceded von Rad's. One of these,
a pamphlet by Hermann Gunkel, is of merely anecdotal interest.
Gunkel was a leading figure in Old Testament research, and he is
the first scholar von Rad names in his *Holy War*. Gunkel's book
on "heroism and war piety in the Old Testament" treated the Old
Testament materials with an eye on Germany and World War I;
he dedicated the book to his son, Werner Gunkel, a soldier in the
German army.[26] Gunkel's thesis was that the existence of nations
and states depends upon the proficiency of their fighting youth.
For that reason, military virtues must pervade the consciousness
of the whole nation.

> As long as a nation preserves faith in itself and its future, as long
> as the spirit of heroic self-sacrifice for the good of the fatherland
> remains alive within it, then it is, even under the most severe
> circumstances, invincible.[27]

This thesis guided Gunkel's meditation on the Old Testament's
view of war. His goal was to interpret the history of Israel as the
spirit of heroism, but Israel's heroism was "the heroism of the

---

von Rad was more interested than the sociologist Weber in locating holy war
within an institution (cf. de Pury, 12). Weber's restricted use of the term "holy
war" accords with the practice of Greek amphictyonies, as these are described by
Smend, 33-34.

25. Cf. von Rad's discussion in *Holy War*, 41-42 (where he speaks of a
"general picture," rather than an ideal type). Talcott Parsons offers a brief description and critique of Weber's ideal type in his introduction to Weber's *Theory*, 3-86
(see esp. 12-13).

26. *Israelitisches Heldentum und Kriegesfrömmigkeit im Alten Testament*
(Göttingen: Vandenhoeck & Ruprecht, 1916).

27. P. 1.

sword and the heroism of faith." In combination, these would make Germany, too, invincible.[28]

While Gunkel's tract contributed little distinctive to the study of holy war, it is at least interesting to note that it was published, as were the studies of Weber and von Rad, during or immediately following a war of considerable consequence to Germany.

The same is true of two other studies, those of the Scandinavian scholars Johannes Pedersen (in 1940) and Henning Fredriksson (in 1945). Pedersen drew on a notion of primitive psychology, a strong feeling of corporate "psychic" unity among ancient Israelites, to explain various phenomena in Israel's life and culture, including its particular understanding of warfare. "All life in Israel," he said, "depends on the interaction of the psychic forces of the people," who are one great "unity of soul."[29] This was especially true in the case of war, and—like Wellhausen—Pedersen viewed ancient Israel as "one great host of warriors."[30] Pedersen followed his predecessors in stressing the religious and cultic aspects of war, but he interpreted these in terms of Israel's effort to create and maintain "that state of increased psychic strength which is requisite in war."[31] In other words, the cultic rites associated in Israel with war could be explained without remainder in terms of psychic forces—von Rad says of Pedersen's view that it portrays holy war "as a great magical network of powers."[32] Pedersen conceived "peace" as consisting in "psychic equilibrium," and war as an activity aimed at restoring that equilibrium. War was, thus, a psychic contest, with each of the competing armies a psychic organism.[33] Rules of holiness surrounding war

28. P. 25.
29. *Israel, Its Life and Culture,* 3-4 (1940; repr. London: Oxford University Press, 1963): 1, 7.
30. P. 2.
31. P. 8.
32. *Holy War,* 70.
33. Pedersen, 20.

protected the warriors from contamination, which would detract from their psychic unity and strength.

Both Weber and Pedersen sought to ground explanations of Israelite warfare, including its ritual and ideological components, in an overarching explanatory framework. Whereas Weber had interpreted Israel in terms of social cohesion guarded by covenant obligations, Pedersen said that there was no "external framework," but only a "psychic unity," keeping the tribes together.[34] Weber's foundational appeal to a feature of Israel's own self-conception, the covenant, and his description of the changing social roles of particular agents (especially prophets), lends his account a persuasiveness lacking in Pedersen's, with its description of war as a "psychic contest." The notion mystifies more than it explains.[35]

The work of Henning Fredriksson marked a departure from all that had gone before. He was not interested in ancient Israelite warfare, in its history or practice, or in its ritual and ideological dimensions. Fredriksson's focus was rather on the *image* of God— the way the Old Testament represents God as a warrior.[36] It does so in two different ways, Fredriksson observed. First, the Old Testament represents Yahweh as the commander of armies. Yahweh comes to the aid of Israel in military conflicts as the leader of Israel's army—or, in the prophets, Yahweh leads foreign armies against Israel. Sometimes the forces Yahweh commands are other than human; they are sometimes natural or cosmic forces, for example. Second, the Old Testament represents Yahweh as a solitary warrior, fighting alone, using various weapons against foes ranging from enemy nations to the forces of chaos. Fredriksson did not attempt to give his survey of images historical or socio-

---

34. P. 7.

35. Pedersen's treatment, apart from its "mystifying" framework, is firmly within mainstream biblical scholarship and contains many instructive observations about war in Israel—or about the views of war in Israelite tradition.

36. *Jahwe als Krieger: Studien zum alttestamentlichen Gottesbild* (Lund: C. W. K. Gleerup, 1945), 3-4.

logical depth. He did argue, however, that the image of Yahweh as a warrior battling against chaos was a late development, deriving from Babylonian influences of the exilic period.[37] And he also claimed that the variably specific ways in which the Old Testament traditions represented Yahweh as a warrior were determined by their general concept of God, concepts that changed significantly over time.[38] It is open to question whether the determination ran in this direction or the reverse, or even whether any such judgments can be made without careful consideration of historical and social factors.[39] Gerhard von Rad tried, in his own way, to consider them.

II

In complete agreement with Wellhausen and Schwally, von Rad emphasizes the religious and cultic character of warfare in ancient Israel, as well as the central importance of holy war in the development of Israel's religious traditions. He agrees with Schwally and Weber that holy war was a covenant affair, situated in the specific cultic and political arrangements of Israel's tribes. With Pedersen, von Rad stresses the importance of religious rituals in preparation for war and in the conduct of war itself. And he agrees with Weber that the prophetic movement was principally responsible for preserving the holy war tradition as a conscious alternative to the theology and practice of the royal court. The distinctive approach von Rad took to the question of holy war in Israel assumes this prior history of research, but von Rad reconceived the question in terms of work he was doing on other matters.

37. Pp. 78, 110.

38. P. 109.

39. E.g., Weber had explained "monolatry" on the basis of early Israel's "undifferentiated culture" (*Ancient Judaism,* 138). Norman K. Gottwald explains Yahwism as a "servomechanism" of early Israel's "egalitarian social-action system" and thus "as a symbolic facilitator of the kind of social interaction which the system prized highly . . ." (*The Tribes of Yahweh: A Sociology of the Religion of Liberated Israel, 1250-1050 B.C.E.* [Maryknoll, N.Y.: Orbis, 1979], 646).

Especially in three areas—form criticism of the Hexateuch, Israelite historiography, and the book of Deuteronomy—von Rad's earlier work provided crucial background to his study of holy war. We can turn to these in order.

A. Form Criticism

Holy War in Ancient Israel is methodologically dependent on form criticism. Von Rad makes this clear in the opening sentence of his book: "Work on the Old Testament today is largely determined by the question of institutions."[40] This question, or inquiry, has its place in the form criticism pioneered by Hermann Gunkel, and von Rad's *Holy War* is a form- and tradition-critical inquiry. He prepared the way for this inquiry in a number of earlier studies, especially "The Form-critical Problem of the Hexateuch."[41] The goal of this essay was to explain the growth of the Hexateuch in a way that accounted for the whole, rather than only for smaller units or traditions. Von Rad agreed with previous scholars that the Hexateuch consists of both literary sources or documents and originally independent traditions that those sources had taken up. But in his view, these scholars had failed to account for the Hexateuch as a whole, and he believed a form-critical analysis could do just that. Von Rad found the key to lie in a series of brief historical creeds in Deuteronomy and Joshua (Deut. 26:5b-9; 6:20-24; Josh. 24:2b-13). He argued that creedal statements like these constituted "a Hexateuch in miniature" and that they provided its

40. *Holy War,* 39. In his approach to Old Testament literature and Israelite history, von Rad was greatly indebted to his own teacher, Albrecht Alt. Alt's most important studies are collected in *Essays on Old Testament History and Religion* (Oxford: Basil Blackwell, 1966, and Garden City: Doubleday, 1968).

41. *The Problem of the Hexateuch,* 1-78; first published in *BWANT* 78 [4/26] (1938). In von Rad's view, the account of the Conquest in Joshua fits together with the five books of the Torah to form the Hexateuch. Joshua is included by most contemporary scholars within the scope of the Deuteronomistic history. Rolf Rendtorff provides a convenient summary in *The Old Testament: An Introduction* (Philadelphia: Fortress, 1986), 183-88.

primary organizing principle by recapitulating "the principal facts of God's redemptive activity."[42] The Yahwist then used this organizing principle to draw together originally disparate traditions into a coherent historical narrative, in which the Settlement tradition has a preeminent place. Behind the traditions themselves, which gathered around the historical creeds, is a long process of growth and development, but it was one individual—the Yahwist—who first joined the traditions and tradition complexes into a single literary work.[43]

Two parts of von Rad's argument about the Hexateuch lay important groundwork for his work in *Holy War*. First, he situates the brief creedal statements in the cult. That is, von Rad proposes that these statements and the traditions associated with them had an institutional *Sitz im Leben*—a setting in the life of ancient Israel—and that setting was the cult. More specifically, von Rad argues that the version of the creed preserved in Deut. 26 shows that the Settlement tradition had its setting in a specific cultic occasion, the ritual of "firstfruits." And he concludes from this that the creedal summary in Deut. 26:5b-9 "is the cult legend of the Feast of Weeks—that is, it contains those elements of Yahwistic faith which were celebrated at the Feast of Weeks." And, "by the use of the creed, the congregation acknowledges the redemptive sovereignty of Yahweh, now seen as the giver of the cultivable land."[44] This conjunction of ritual and ideological dimensions, situated in a specific institutional setting—and even a specific site, Gilgal—reflects exactly what von Rad means by "the question of institutions"[45] in his study of holy war. Holy war is not merely a

---

42. "The Form-critical Problem of the Hexateuch," 8, 4. Cf. Douglas A. Knight, *Rediscovering the Traditions of Israel*. SBL Dissertation 9 (Missoula: Scholars Press, 1973), 99.

43. For a recent evaluation, see Douglas A. Knight, "The Pentateuch," *The Hebrew Bible and Its Modern Interpreters,* ed. Knight and Gene M. Tucker (Philadelphia: Fortress and Chico: Scholars Press, 1985), 293-96.

44. "The Form-critical Problem of the Hexateuch," 43.

45. *Holy War,* 39.

tradition, according to von Rad, but is also a particular institution; these two, tradition and institution, always go together. It is in part for this reason that von Rad argues that holy wars were defensive battles fought during the period of the judges. They cannot be set in the time of the Exodus or Settlement, because even though some kind of cultic organization is possible for the tribes in that earlier period, we can know nothing for certain of their worship. A cultic tradition, which von Rad claims holy war to be, presupposes a cultic institution. It presupposes the amphictyony, and we can know nothing of any amphictyony prior to the period of the judges.[46]

Second, the Yahwist's narrative appropriation of originally cultic traditions as literature reflects exactly what happened, according to von Rad, in the case of the holy war tradition. The traditions preserved in the Hexateuch became detached from their setting in the cult and were thereby free to be spiritualized. Von Rad points to an example of this spiritualization in the Priestly version of the manna story in Exod. 16. Whereas the Yahwistic version still bears the marks of a story,

> the priestly account is very different. The incident is ostensibly presented as a wholly factual matter, but in such a way that no reader will dwell upon the externals, and all can readily grasp the hidden spiritual import. The miracle, which took place at a particular time and place, has been generalised and has become something of virtually timeless validity.[47]

The difference between the two versions is that between a story-teller and a theologian. And, von Rad says, a corollary of spiritu-

---

46. *Holy War,* 56. By "amphictyony" von Rad means the cultic and political organization of the twelve tribes in the premonarchic period. He took the term and much of his understanding of Israel's tribal association from Martin Noth, *Das System der zwölf Stämme Israels.* BWANT 52 [4/1] (1930; repr. Stuttgart: Kohlhammer, 1966). In *Holy War* von Rad assumes a distinction between institution and *Sitz im Leben,* with holy war being the institution and the cult its *Sitz im Leben.* That setting, of course, made of holy war a specifically cultic institution.

47. "The Form-critical Problem of the Hexateuch," 49.

alization is rationalization. By this he means that a theologian—
a Priestly or a Deuteronomic theologian, for example—"is no
longer in the position of an awestruck unsophisticated recipient of
the material, but begins to take control of it and to shape it according to the needs of his own reason."[48] This is just what happened in the case of holy war tradition: it became literature. In the
period of the judges, holy war was a cultic institution; but once
the tradition of holy war became dissociated from the cult, it was
free to be taken up, as literature, within large narrative compositions. Just as in the case of the hexateuchal traditions, the holy
war tradition *as literature* was spiritualized and rationalized: it was
used to serve theological ends quite different from those it served
in its original cultic setting.[49]

B. The Solomonic Enlightenment

It was Israel's historical writing that signalled most clearly, for
von Rad, just this distinction between an "awestruck unsophisticated" storyteller and a spiritualizing, rationalizing theologian. In
a survey of Israelite historiography, published in 1944, von Rad
observed that "only a political state which *makes* history can *write*
history."[50] This laconic observation points to a crucial distinction
between the "hero-sagas" from the amphictyonic period—the period of genuine holy war—and the historical writing produced
during the Monarchy. The change from a tribal confederacy or
amphictyony to a monarchy involved more than just political and
economic arrangements; important as these were, the intellectual
or spiritual changes were just as profound. Von Rad associates the
most decisive changes with Solomon: "the time of Solomon was

48. "The Form-critical Problem of the Hexateuch," 49.
49. He discusses this process in *Holy War,* 81-93.
50. "The Beginnings of Historical Writing in Ancient Israel," *The Problem
of the Hexateuch,* 192. For more recent developments in the study of Israelite
historiography, see Baruch Halpern, *The First Historians: The Hebrew Bible and
History* (San Francisco: Harper & Row, 1988).

a period of 'Enlightenment,' of a sharp break with the ancient patriarchal code of living."[51] This enlightenment under Solomon meant a diminished interest in the cult and in the sacral dimension of life generally, in favor of "the realm of the profane."[52] It included a new openness to foreign cultural influences, to international wisdom and "secular ideas,"[53] and it included especially an interest in human affairs and *human agency* in the course of those affairs.

This interest in human activity, and the corresponding emphasis on human agency, represented a significant difference between history writing influenced by the Solomonic enlightenment and the earlier hero-sagas. In narratives of the latter sort, in the crucial moment, "God intervenes to act and to deliver," and "human co-operation is not called for." "It is God's miraculous activity in history which is glorified."[54] Genuine history writing, after the enlightenment, continued to relate divine and human activity, but in a vastly different way—in a way that emphasized human agency. Here God does not intervene miraculously, taking the action away from the protagonists; rather, Israel's first enlightenment historian—the author of the Throne Succession narrative—portrayed God's activity as hidden, as working providentially in human affairs and through human agents. Von Rad speaks in this connection of "the *concursus divinus* which makes it possible for our historian to do justice to human effectiveness in his presentation of human activities."[55] Divine cooperation, rather than intervention, marks off history writing from hero sagas.

The Solomonic enlightenment—he also speaks of "Solo-

---

51. "Beginnings of Historical Writing," 203.
52. "Beginnings of Historical Writing," 202.
53. "Beginnings of Historical Writing," 203. Von Rad's exemplar for Israelite historiography under the Solomonic enlightenment is the Throne Succession narrative in 2 Sam. 9–20; 1 Kgs. 1–2.
54. "Beginnings of Historical Writing," 174, 176. Von Rad is here commenting on Judg. 7:2-8.
55. "Beginnings of Historical Writing," 201.

monic humanism"—plays a decisive role, half a decade later, in von Rad's *Holy War*. The narratives in Judges and 1 Samuel recounting the wars of Israel's tribal confederacy are themselves far removed from that period and from its cult. They are works of literature from after the Solomonic enlightenment, when the cultic tradition of holy war had been incorporated in a theologically sophisticated literature. To capture the differences more exactly, von Rad contrasts the Solomonic enlightenment with the "pan-sacralism" of the amphictyonic period that preceded it. One important feature of the earlier pan-sacralism was its belief that Yahweh intervened in historical events. In fact, von Rad claims that trust in Yahweh's intervention had its origin precisely in holy war.[56] By contrast, Israel's enlightened historiography viewed Yahweh's action as one of cooperation with human agents, and it was historians of this view who preserved the holy war traditions as literature. That explains, for von Rad, why the holy war accounts in the Old Testament do not preserve the cultic institutional setting and character that he believes holy war must have had, and which the amphictyony provided. That setting and character—and pan-sacralism itself—gave way to the enlightenment. For that reason, the institution of holy war has to be reconstructed from texts that preserve it in only fragmentary fashion.

It is just here that von Rad's own account is most complex. It would seem, on the basis of his discussion of historiography, that von Rad would attribute the emphasis on Yahweh's direct and decisive intervention in holy war to the amphictyonic period itself, pre-enlightenment. Instead, he does just the reverse. According to the ideology of holy war, he says, Yahweh and Israel acted together in a kind of "synergism," a term he borrowed from Martin Buber.[57] The narratives emphasizing Yahweh's own action, and crediting Yahweh alone with victory in war, are the product of enlightenment thinking after Solomon. It seems, then, that von Rad exactly

---

56. *Holy War,* 70.
57. *Holy War,* 49.

reversed himself in the few years intervening between his studies of historiography and of holy war. His own explanation is more complex. In the amphictyonic period, von Rad says, Yahweh's intervention was decisive, and the pan-sacralism of that period enabled Israel to think of the relation of this decisive intervention to human agency as unproblematic. Later, however, under the enlightenment's influence, this relation was itself a matter for theological reflection. But instead of playing down Yahweh's singular intervention, enlightenment historians emphasized it all the more. They did so not in the interest of recounting an ancient institution and its crucial events but in order to describe the faith that Yahweh's miracle elicited from its witnesses, and thus to appeal to the faith of a later community. This appeal to the faith of individuals, nowhere more obvious than in Exod. 14:13b-14, 30-31,[58] reflects precisely the humanism of Solomon's enlightenment; while it highlighted the miraculous aspects of holy war—even drawing a contrast between them and any element of human cooperation—it had no real interest in miracle at all. Its interest was in confession—confession of faith, "so that Israel might believe."[59] In his reconstruction of the institution of holy war, von Rad looks behind this theological reflection, and behind its enlightenment concerns, to a more primitive and sacral Israel, when miracle was a part of the event itself and not a literary topic with a spiritual lesson.

58. *Holy War,* 89.
59. *Holy War,* 91. This does not entirely eliminate contradictions between von Rad's arguments in "Beginnings of Historical Writing" and those in *Holy War.* For example, in "Beginnings of Historical Writing" he says that the portrayal of God's intervention at the climactic moment of Gideon's battle, in Judg. 7, is characteristic of hero sagas; but "this does not happen in historical writing" (174). Commenting on the same text in *Holy War,* he says that "we first encounter here in the work of these post-Solomonic novella writers that understanding by which holy war and the absolute miracle of Yahweh are inseparably bound—indeed, are one and the same thing" (87). It would seem that von Rad cannot hold both opinions simultaneously without contradicting himself. See also *Old Testament Theology* (New York: Harper & Row and Edinburgh: Oliver & Boyd, 1962), 1:328-29.

C. Deuteronomy

His form-critical study of the Hexateuch and his survey of Israelite historiography laid the methodological and historical foundations of von Rad's argument in *Holy War.* But a significant question remains: if holy war was an institution of Israel's amphictyonic era, why does it appear only in the (Deuteronomic) literature of a much later period? His *Studies in Deuteronomy*, written in 1945-1946, provided von Rad an answer. In those studies, von Rad concludes that the book of Deuteronomy had its provenance "within Judah's revived militia."[60] In the years after 701 B.C.E., the decline of Assyria's power over the west, including Judah, provided both the opportunity and the need for such a revival. It was a revival sponsored not only by the royal court but by country Levites; they proclaimed the old amphictyonic or patriarchal traditions "of the strict Jahweh faith" that had "long remained alive amongst the free peasant population, and given rise to an opposition to the capital which expressed itself in strong impulses towards revival both in the cult and in politics."[61] In the 6th cent., these impulses took political form in a campaign for national independence and internal reform, in that way situating the institution of holy war once again within its cultic setting. According to von Rad, this explains the strongly martial character of Deuteronomy, including its explicit references to war (Deut. 20:1-20; 21:10-14; 23:10-14; 24:5; 25:17-19), and its association of war with the cult. This was not Deuteronomy's invention; to the contrary, Deuteronomy revived an ancient amphictyonic tradition in

60. *Studies in Deuteronomy*, 61. Von Rad had written an earlier book on Deuteronomy, *Das Gottesvolk im Deuteronomium. BWANT* 47 [3/11] (Stuttgart: Kohlhammer, 1929), of which he says that *Studies in Deuteronomy* is, "in substantial points, a correction" (*Studies in Deuteronomy*, 59 n. 3).

61. *Studies in Deuteronomy*, 66. In both *Studies in Deuteronomy* (60-61) and *Holy War* (124-25) von Rad acknowledges his dependence on Erhard Junge for the theory of a revival of holy war practice and ideology following the events of 701 B.C.E. (Erhard Junge, *Der Wiederaufbau des Herrwesens des Reiches Juda unter Josia. BWANT* 75 [4/23] [Stuttgart: Kohlhammer, 1937]).

much later circumstances—not for theological purposes alone, but for the purpose of restoring the amphictyonic militia itself. At the same time, Deuteronomy's author had to reckon with the possibility that his audience would have a "conception of warlike events" very different from that of holy war and its exclusive reliance on Yahweh.[62] For that reason, Deuteronomy joined its retrieval of holy war with a theology that stressed, in an apologetic and sometimes rationalizing way, Israel's need to rely on Yahweh alone.

His investigation of Deuteronomy serves von Rad well in *Holy War*. Specifically, it enables him to explain the reappearance, at a very late date in Judah's monarchical history, of a tradition whose institutional life ended centuries earlier with Solomon. However, von Rad also notes that it reappeared in altered character. Ancient Israel's holy wars were defensive—in defense of the amphictyony—while Deuteronomy conceives them primarily as wars of religion; it thus reverses, in this sense, the ancient tradition it revived.[63] How did this reversal come about? Von Rad does not pursue this question; he seems to see its explanation in the circles that preserved the memory of holy war, namely the conservative agricultural circles outside the capital: the "people of the land." But he also notes that after the royal court took over control of the military and its strategy, it was the prophets who, in the 9th cent., became "the bearers and the proclaimers of traditions that have already almost died out among the people."[64]

Just as Max Weber had done earlier, von Rad views the early prophets as bearers of an alternative and even underground tradition—a tradition that sponsored faith in Yahweh alone, in self-

---

62. *Studies in Deuteronomy,* 56. Von Rad makes the same observation in *Holy War,* commenting on Deut. 9:1-6, which he locates in the context of holy war: "the warning against self praise shows that the speaker is reckoning throughout with the possibility of a very secular understanding of the events of war" (122-23).

63. *Holy War,* 72-73, 117-18.

64. *Holy War,* 98. Von Rad discusses the social and religious effects of Israel's transition to monarchy in *Old Testament Theology,* 1:44, 59-60, 317.

conscious contrast to the pragmatic planning of the royal court. That faith took a somewhat different form—but still in explicit relation to holy war—in the 8th-cent. prophet Isaiah, who followed the enlightenment historians in drawing an absolute contrast between Yahweh's action and human participation. Isaiah uttered this call to faith in direct challenge to his secularized contemporaries, in a situation of continuing national emergency, and in that way ascribed to war the character of a religious test.[65] Recall that Weber understood all genuine holy wars to be wars of religion, and that he took this tradition of religious holy war to be what the prophets preserved underground. Had von Rad followed Weber more closely in this regard, he might have been able to draw a closer connection between the ancient institution and its revival in Deuteronomy. However, it was particularly his studies of the Hexateuch, Israelite historiography, and the book of Deuteronomy that led von Rad to judgments different from those of Weber and his other predecessors on the question of holy war.

III

As I said at the beginning, von Rad's theory of holy war seemingly accounts for everything. Its coherence depends in large part on the existence of a tribal confederation, of both political and cultic dimensions, to provide the setting for the institution of holy war as he reconstructs it. In other words, von Rad has to reconstruct or assume *both* the institution of holy war *and* the amphictyony in which it was set. The first extensive criticism of von Rad's *Holy War* concentrated on that very relation of holy war to the amphictyony. In *Yahweh War and Tribal War,* first published in 1963, Rudolf

---

65. *Holy War,* 102-3. Von Rad compares Isaiah in this respect with Exod. 14. He sees in Exod. 14 a narrator "teaching in an edifying way," while in Isaiah a prophet "in real distress wants to prepare the way for the miracle through his call to faith" (103). See also von Rad's comments on Isaiah in *Old Testament Theology* 2 (1965): 159-160.

Smend concluded that the amphictyony prior to Samuel was a cultic association, and not primarily political or military. Early Israel's wars were not a function of any cultic institution, despite the ritual features accompanying them,[66] and for that reason it is improper, Smend argued, to speak of "holy war"; we should instead speak of "Yahweh war." Incidents of warfare in early Israel involved only individual tribes or tribal associations formed for war and then disbanded; they did not involve the entire amphictyony, and they certainly did not do so in any institutional sense. However, because it was Yahweh, the God of all Israel, who fought on behalf of a tribe or group of tribes, Yahweh war contained an impulse toward the kind of political unity that resulted in the Israelite state. That impulse was channeled through the amphictyony, but war was never an institution of the amphictyony and was not a cultic event.[67]

Smend thus called into question the major component of von Rad's theory: that holy war was a cultic institution of the amphictyony. Nonetheless, Smend's criticisms left intact the notion of early Israel's organization in an amphictyony. Smend argues, in dependence on Martin Noth, that the amphictyony originally included only six tribes, the "sons of Leah." It was the "sons of Rachel"—the tribes of Joseph and Benjamin—who brought with them into the tribal league a distinctive experience of the wars of Yahweh.[68] Those tribes carried the memory of Israel's deliverance from Egypt, which was the first war of Yahweh. In that case, Yahweh war would have preceded the amphictyony and "would have actually been the original element of what in time was destined to become the religion of Israel."[69] Finally then, in Smend's view,

66. Smend, 36-37.
67. Smend, 40-42. Cf. Gwilym H. Jones, " 'Holy War' or 'Yahweh War'?" *VT* 25 (1975): 642-658.
68. Smend, 105-7. As Manfred Weippert notes, Smend's account of the Israelite tribes and their warfare is here closer to Martin Noth's view than is von Rad's, although von Rad relied heavily on Noth's description of the amphictyony (Weippert, 464-65; cf. Martin Noth, *The History of Israel*, 2nd ed. [New York: Harper & Row, 1960], 105-6).
69. Smend, 134.

Yahweh war and the amphictyony are related, but in such a way that the latter could not have been the institutional setting of the former.

If Smend's arguments suggested adjustments to von Rad's theory of holy war, later studies called for a more radical reevaluation. Manfred Weippert's investigation of "holy war" in Israel and Assyria made the very notion of holy war seem an anachronism: there is no basis in ancient texts, Weippert claimed, for maintaining a distinction between holy and profane wars.[70] Furthermore, Weippert argued that none of the ritual and ideological components of von Rad's theory of holy war were in any way unique to Israel; to the contrary, they were part of the practice and ideology of war common in the ancient Near East and probably in all of antiquity. In Israel itself there was no distinction in principle between the charismatic leadership of war in the period of the confederacy, on the one hand, and its conduct under the monarchy, on the other. And finally, the institution of a professional army did not mean the elimination of the tribal militia.[71] Weippert omitted any explicit criticism of von Rad's reconstruction of the holy war tradition; he concentrated instead on von Rad's proposed *theory* of holy war, in its ritual and ideological components. Even so, it is clear that Weippert deprived von Rad's form-critical and tradition-historical investigation of its rationale. That rationale consisted in the possibility of reconstructing an institution that differed sharply from later historical realities. If no such institution as holy war ever existed, efforts to reconstruct it will be pointless.

That is the conclusion Fritz Stolz drew, in a thorough inves-

70. Weippert, 490. See above, n. 10. Moshe Weinfeld has collected a broader range of comparative material from the ancient Near East, around the topic of divine intervention in war ("Divine Intervention in War in Ancient Israel and in the Ancient Near East," *History, Historiography and Interpretation,* ed. Hayim Tadmor and Weinfeld [Jerusalem: Magnes, 1983], 121-147).

71. Weippert, 490-92. Weippert grants a certain legitimacy to the term "Yahweh war," so long as it remains clear that the relation between Yahweh and Israel's wars was not different in principle from that between Mesopotamian deities and Assyria's wars (490).

tigation published the same year as Weippert's essay, 1972.[72] Stolz's was the first comprehensive treatment of "Yahweh war" in Israel, and it remains the only one. It stands, then, as a counterpoint to von Rad's *Holy War,* reflecting changes in two intervening decades of Old Testament scholarship. Stolz does not assume an amphictyony, even in Rudolf Smend's modified sense, and he denies that the Israelite tribes shared any common experience of war. At the beginning of Israel's history, Stolz claims, there was no homogeneous institution of holy war; instead, there was only wide diversity. The tribes did share experiences of "Yahweh war," crediting Yahweh with victory over militarily superior forces, but these wars shared no common pattern, ritual or ideological; there was no common vocabulary for describing them, and no common cultic or political setting.[73] Lacking these, there can be no appeal to an ancient institution of holy war, reflected in texts whose authors or redactors no longer knew of it, to explain the typical schema of "holy war" in those texts of Deuteronomy, Joshua, and Judges. This typical schema, consisting of the vocabulary and themes that von Rad lists at the beginning of *Holy War,*[74] forms the basis of Stolz's investigation. As von Rad admits, the schema of holy war is preserved in late, Deuteronomic texts. Stolz takes

---

72. *Jahwes und Israels Kriege.* Abhandlungen zur Theologie des Alten und Neuen Testaments 60 (Zurich: Theologischer Verlag, 1972). Wolfgang Richter's earlier studies in the book of Judges played an important role in reconceiving Israel's premonarchic period and particularly the traditions about it. Richter's influence is apparent in Stolz's work. See Wolfgang Richter, *Traditionsgeschichtliche Untersuchung zur Richterbuch.* Bonner biblische Beiträge 18 (Bonn: Hanstein, 1963); *Die Bearbeitung des 'Retterbuches' in der deuteronomischen Epoche.* Bonner biblische Beiträge 21 (Bonn: Hanstein, 1964).

73. See Stolz's summary, 196-205. The view that Israel lacked a central sanctuary, and thus a *Sitz im Leben* for any common tradition, in the tribal or "prenational" period has become widespread. Cf., e.g., Niels Peter Lemche, *Early Israel: Anthropological and Historical Studies on the Israelite Society Before the Monarchy.* VTS 37 (Leiden: Brill, 1985), 303, and the literature he cites there. Cf. J. Maxwell Miller and John H. Hayes, *A History of Ancient Israel and Judah* (Philadelphia: Westminster, 1986), 107-9.

74. Pp. 41-51.

this fact very seriously and concludes that the holy war schema, the very theory of holy war, is itself the invention of the Deuteronomic theologians: it is a literary and theological fiction.

Stolz does not deny that Israel experienced "Yahweh war" early in its history. He does insist, however, that these experiences of Yahweh's triumph in war were diverse and that the development of a uniform holy war schema can be traced in the history of Israelite literature, and even in the development of the book of Deuteronomy itself. Later texts in Deuteronomy (e.g., Deut. 1:30; 3:22) emphasize more strongly than its earlier ones (e.g., 7:21; 9:3) Yahweh's presence and activity in Israel's wars. And later levels of the Deuteronomic tradition speak in greater detail and "more theoretically" of Yahweh war than do its earlier ones.[75] The manner in which the Deuteronomistic historians incorporated earlier stories into their theory and literary schema of holy war can be illustrated by comparing Num. 21:21-26 with Deut. 2:26-37.[76] The former text describes, in spare detail, an attack by the Amorite king Sihon against Israel, designed to prevent them from passing through his territory. There was a battle, Israel prevailed, and the Israelites occupied the former Amorite territory. There is no mention of cultic ritual nor any evidence of holy war (or Yahweh war) ideology; the text does not so much as allude to Yahweh's involvement.[77] By contrast, in Deut. 2, which describes the same event,

---

75. Stolz, 25. At least since Martin Noth's work on the Deuteronomistic history, it has been commonly accepted that Deut. 1–3 (or 1:4–4:40) is from that historical work and is thus later than the Deuteronomic traditions that lie at the core of the book of Deuteronomy. See Noth, *Überlieferungsgeschichtliche Studien 1: Die sammelnden und bearbeitenden Geschichtswerke im Alten Testament,* 2nd ed. (Tübingen: Max Niemeyer, 1957), 14; A. D. H. Mayes, *Deuteronomy.* New Century Bible Commentary (Grand Rapids: Wm. B. Eerdmans and London: Marshall, Morgan & Scott, 1981), 29-55. Jones also sees a historical development *toward* holy war in the history of Israel's traditions (654-55).

76. Stolz himself does not draw this comparison explicitly. See, however, his remarks, 25, 73-74. Cf. Sa-Moon Kang, *Divine War in the Old Testament and in the Ancient Near East.* BZAW 177 (Berlin: de Gruyter, 1989), 127-29.

77. Stolz notes the absence of any mention of Yahweh in Num. 21:21-26 and in the song that follows (vv. 27-30). He suggests that the song originally

the entire panoply of holy war is present, with particular emphasis on Yahweh's deliverance of Sihon into Israel's hands. Rather than preserving or, as von Rad argued, recovering an institution of holy war, the Deuteronomists appear to have reworked earlier traditions from their own theological perspective, of which the holy war schema was a principal expression.

In his discussion of the prophets and holy war, von Rad argues that Isaiah's rejection of armaments and alliances, his "motif of looking to Yahweh and of standing still," and his idea of faith all derived from the holy war tradition—particularly as it is exemplified in Exod. 14.[78] At the same time, von Rad was puzzled about Isaiah: "What . . . remains temporarily unexplained is the question of how the old tradition [of holy war] can have stood so much in the center for this one prophet, whereas other prophets seem not to know it."[79] On Stolz's account, an explanation is at hand. Isaiah is unique among the prophets in his dependence on the Zion tradition centered in and on the city of Jerusalem and celebrated in its cult. In his investigation of this Jerusalem cult tradition, especially as preserved in 1 Kgs. 8 and several psalms (e.g., Pss. 10, 18, 24, 47, 68, 80, 132), Stolz observes that Yahweh is revered in Jerusalem as a God of war: Yahweh stands with the people in time of need, and secures them against cosmic and historical enemies. Yahweh's presence in Jerusalem is connected especially by the ark, and the epithets of Yahweh associated with it—"Yahweh of hosts" and "enthroned upon the cherubim"—

---

celebrated a "profane" war but was later understood as a "Yahweh war-song" (74). Cf. also Gwilym H. Jones, "The Concept of Holy War," *The World of Ancient Israel*, ed. Ronald E. Clements (Cambridge: Cambridge University Press, 1989), 308. However, the song may well have originated in non-Israelite circles. Cf. Paul D. Hanson, "The Song of Heshbon and David's *Nîr*," *Harvard Theological Review* 61 (1968): 297-320; Gottwald, 215 (and 738 n. 153).

78. *Holy War*, 107, 108. Von Rad devotes greater attention to the prophets in his later essay, "The Origin of the Concept of the Day of Yahweh," *Journal of Semitic Studies* 4 (1959): 97-108. There he argues that the prophets took the notion of the "day of Yahweh" from old holy war tradition, but broadened it to include the universal and even cosmic sphere. Cf. *Old Testament Theology*, 2:123-24.

79. *Holy War*, 114.

symbolize Yahweh's rule over, and defense of, both cosmic order and the Davidic empire as its guardian.[80] A tradition that emphasized Yahweh's singular power and ascribed credit for victory to Yahweh alone consequently stressed human powerlessness. While Stolz finds evidence of this in the Psalms (e.g., Ps. 20:6-7; 44:3, 6-7; 60:11-12), the clearest examples are in Isaiah (Isa. 30:15-16; 31:1, 3).[81] In other words, exactly those features of Isaiah that distinguish the book, and which von Rad traced back to holy war, Stolz finds at home in the Jerusalem tradition. Von Rad's question, why Isaiah is unique among the prophets in his dependence on holy war, is easily answered on Stolz's account: Isaiah did not depend on the tradition of holy war or Yahweh war but on that of the Jerusalem cult.[82]

Stolz does not deny a relation between Isaiah and Yahweh war; rather, he conceives that relation to run exactly opposite to the direction von Rad had proposed. The cultic tradition preserved in Jerusalem, with its ritual celebration of Yahweh's power and conquest of historical and cosmic foes (e.g., in Ps. 24), constitutes the principal source of the Yahweh war tradition. That source was mediated through the Deuteronomistic history, which united a wide variety of historical narratives and traditions of conquest and settlement with mythological and liturgical—but in all events, theological—traditions at home in Jerusalem. Stolz acknowledges that belief in Yahweh as a warrior who fights in defense of Israel is as old as Israel itself. That belief grew out of Israel's diverse experience of deliverance in war, and it assumed a particular shape in the theology and liturgy of Jerusalem's cult, as well as in the royal court. With the distinctive themes of the Jerusalem tradition and

---

80. Stolz, 29-45.

81. P. 117. Stolz acknowledges that the motif of Yahweh's power contrasted with "human powerlessness" *(menschliche Ohnmacht)* occurs also in Hosea (Hos. 10:13; 14:3), where it cannot have depended on the Jerusalem cult tradition (118). Its origins are thus earlier than any of the later Israelite tradition complexes (119).

82. I have argued similarly in *Zion, The City of the Great King.* JSOT Supplement 41 (Sheffield: JSOT Press, 1987), 100-104.

such symbols as the ark, the Deuteronomists brought together a history that depicted in narrative form the wars of Yahweh on behalf of Israel.[83]

Recent research has tended to emphasize, with Stolz, the mythological dimensions, and even origins, of Israel's conceptions of Yahweh war. For example, H. H. Schmid highlights the conception of peace *(shalom)*, particularly at home in the Jerusalem cult traditions, as the proper background against which to understand the Yahweh war narratives: war was aimed at the restoration of peace.[84] Frank Moore Cross and Patrick D. Miller, Jr., have examined the mythological background of Yahweh war, or holy war, from a different direction, primarily through an analysis of Israel's earliest poetry.[85] These poems portray Yahweh as the divine warrior who battles against cosmic foes for the order of the world, but in so doing, and at the same time, Yahweh battles on behalf of Israel and against its historical enemies. In this way, the mythology of Yahweh as divine warrior and Israel's experience of holy war are conflated.[86]

83. Stolz cites Exod. 14 as an example of a Yahweh war text that shows influence from both the Jerusalem cult tradition and the Deuteronomists (94-97). He ascribes it to a redactional layer of the Yahwistic source (96). Jean-Louis Ska has criticized Stolz's argument on this point, in "Exode xiv contient-il un récit de 'guerre sainte' de style deutéronomistique?" *VT* 33 (1983): 454-467.

84. "Heiliger Krieg und Gottesfrieden im Alten Testament," *Altorientalische Welt in der alttestamentlichen Theologie* (Zurich: Theologischer Verlag, 1972), 91-120. Cf. Odil H. Steck, *Friedensvorstellungen im alten Jerusalem: Psalmen, Jesaja, Deuterojesaja.* Theologische Studien 111 (Zurich: Theologischer Verlag, 1972).

85. Cross, *Canaanite Myth and Hebrew Epic* (Cambridge, Mass.: Harvard University Press, 1973); Miller, *The Divine Warrior in Early Israel.*

86. Cf. Patrick D. Miller, Jr., 161-62. I have argued against this conflation in *Zion, The City of the Great King,* 101-2. An example of the confusion to which it can lead is provided by Cross in his criticism of von Rad's *Holy War.* Cross criticizes von Rad's description of "Israel's sacral warfare as an institution of the era of the Judges, limited to the defensive wars of Israel." Cross claims that the wars of the Conquest were "the wars of Yahweh par excellence" and that von Rad's view "rests on the dogma" that the Conquest traditions are unhistorical (Cross, 88). This criticism is mistaken. As I have shown above, von Rad speaks not of "sacral warfare" but of a specific cultic institution of holy war, whose setting, he claims, we can only describe for the period of the tribal confederacy.

Taken together, the work of Cross and Miller, on the one hand, expands on and possibly corrects the conclusions of Stolz and Schmid, on the other. Lying behind the holy war or Yahweh war narratives is not only the liturgical tradition of the Jerusalem cult but an even earlier poetic tradition, represented in texts such as Exod. 15; Deut. 33; and Ps. 68, celebrating Yahweh's triumph on Israel's behalf.[87] However, Judg. 5 (the Song of Deborah) is also among these early texts, according to Cross and Miller, and it marks for von Rad the beginning of holy war in Israel. Thus the question of dating these texts becomes crucial for understanding the history of Yahweh war in Israel and the history of its tradition in the Old Testament. If Cross, Miller, and others are right in dating these "divine warrior" poems in the period before David, then the relation among (a) these early poems, (b) the Jerusalem cult tradition, and (c) the narrative accounts of Yahweh war in the Old Testament is more complex than Stolz has seen it to be.[88] Since it seems clear that the poem in Judg. 5 has influenced the Deborah-Barak narrative in Judg. 4, the way is left open for considering more directly a relation between Israel's earliest poetry and its historiography.[89] By the same token, of course, the way is also left open for exploring the relation between these early poems—and later ones as well— and Israel's experiences in war. The way is left open, that is to say, for an investigation of holy war in ancient Israel that attempts to

---

87. Cf. Baruch Halpern, *The Constitution of the Monarchy in Israel.* HSM 25 (Chico: Scholars Press, 1981), 51-109. In some respects, Halpern helps to bridge the gap between the conclusions of Cross and Patrick D. Miller regarding the "divine warrior" and those of Stolz regarding the Jerusalem cult tradition.

88. According to Stolz, Exod. 15 reflects the combining of Exodus and Zion traditions which took place in the Jerusalem cult prior to Deuteronomy (91-94). Stolz also claims that Judg. 5 has its setting in the Jerusalem cult (110).

89. Baruch Halpern has treated the relation between the poetic accounts in Exod. 15 and Judg. 5 and their prose counterparts in Exod. 14 and Judg. 4 in "Doctrine by Misadventure: Between the Israelite Source and the Biblical Historian," *The Poet and the Historian: Essays in Literary and Historical Biblical Criticism*, ed. Richard E. Friedman. Harvard Semitic Studies 26 (Chico: Scholars Press, 1983), 41-73.

be as comprehensive as von Rad was, while taking into account historical and literary complexities that were not apparent when von Rad issued his little book.[90]

In one area, von Rad's conclusions have proved durable, even if they were conclusions anticipated by Max Weber: holy war (or Yahweh war) tradition was an instrument of prophetic criticism against the royal court. This criticism has been interpreted as a conflict between prophets, whose charismatic leadership in war was rendered irrelevant by the monarchy's bureaucratic conduct of war, and the royal court itself.[91] But it has also been seen as a more theologically substantive criticism of the monarchy for ignoring, in practice, the decisive element of holy war: the conviction that victory is achieved by Yahweh. Peter Weimar has explored this prophetic criticism in a lengthy examination of four narratives, Exod. 14; Josh. 10; Judg. 4; and 1 Sam. 7.[92] According to Weimar, these narratives in their earliest form shared a common structure: (a) an enemy takes action against Israel; (b) Israel becomes discouraged; (c) a prophet urges confidence and faith in Yahweh; (d) Yahweh intervenes and puts the enemy to rout; (e) Israel's only action is to pursue the routed enemy.[93] The intention of these

90. In *The Poet and the Historian,* ed. Friedman, Moshe Weinfeld explores the impact of the monarchy, with its institutional ideology, on earlier Israel's ritual and ideology of warfare ("Zion and Jerusalem as Religious and Political Capital: Ideology and Utopia," 75-125). Echoing von Rad, Weinfeld speaks once more of "The Institution of Holy War" (79).

91. In addition to Weber and von Rad, see Richter, *Traditionsgeschichtliche Untersuchung zur Richterbuch,* 61-63; Stolz, 132-154; Jones, "The Concept of Holy War," 315. On the topic generally, see Walter Dietrich, *David, Saul, und die Propheten: Das Verhältnis von Religion und Politik nach den prophetischen Überlieferungen vom frühesten Königtum in Israel. BWANT* 122 (Stuttgart: Kohlhammer, 1987), esp. 51-63.

92. "Die Jahwekriegeserzählungen in Exodus 14, Josua 10, Richter 4 und 1 Samuel 7," *Bibl* 57 (1976): 38-73. Jones, in "The Concept of Holy War," agrees with Weimar (without citing him) that prophetic criticism of the monarchy was important in the development of holy war theory (315).

93. Cf. the summary of Weimar's article in de Pury, 33. The exception to the pattern is Exod. 14, where the enemy is totally destroyed by the sea.

narratives is less historiographic than theological, according to Weimar, and they are earlier than the Deuteronomistic history. Indeed, they come from northern circles brought to Jerusalem in the period of David; they are directed against the royal court, and perhaps against David himself. Their interest in prophetic figures in relation to Yahweh (Moses, Deborah, Samuel) suggests an origin among prophets critical of the religious politics of the Davidic court.[94] In their strong emphasis on Yahweh's sovereign action, these holy war narratives criticize political policies that locate sovereignty elsewhere.

Weimar's conclusions about these four holy war narratives depend on conjectures about their original form and date. However, the most recent comprehensive study of warfare in Israel, by T. R. Hobbs, supports Weimar's contention—and von Rad's—that the prophetic heirs of holy war tradition used it to criticize the political ideology of Israel's kings:

> In the period of the monarchy itself warfare became an instrument of policy and this is seen in the attitudes towards enemies engendered by the royalist ideology . . . In that same period the prophetic champions of the covenant order reacted to the monarchical use of warfare by transforming its conventional literary war poems.[95]

Hobbs demurs from calling the prophetic criticism of warfare "pacifistic," even though de Pury uses exactly this term to characterize the prophetic opposition described by Weimar.[96] Millard C. Lind, in his study *Yahweh Is a Warrior*, would not be as timid. With von Rad, Lind situates the decisive period of holy war in the years prior to the Monarchy; with Cross and Miller, he ascribes a healthy measure of historical reality to the early poems that portray Yahweh as a warrior; and with von Rad, Weimar, and Hobbs, Lind

---

94. Weimar, 72-73.
95. T. R. Hobbs, *A Time for War: A Study of Warfare in the Old Testament.* Old Testament Studies 3 (Wilmington: Michael Glazier, 1989), 198.
96. Hobbs, 196; de Pury, 35.

associates holy war tradition with prophetic leadership in Israel critical of the monarchy and its warfare practices and ideology. But in departure from von Rad and all his successors, Lind finds the normative paradigm of holy war in Exod. 15. Here, in the Old Testament's oldest text, Yahweh alone delivers Israel. Lind considers this to be of a theological piece with the prose narrative in Exod. 14, and with the portrayal of prophetic leadership through Moses in the larger Exodus narrative.[97] Pacifism, construed as politics centered on Yahweh's sovereignty and prophetic leadership of the community, Lind offers as the theological center of the Yahweh war tradition.

According to Lind, the emphasis on Yahweh acting alone to give Israel victory is found at the beginning of the Yahweh war tradition and of Israel's very history; according to von Rad, this emphasis was the product of late theological reflection by enlightened historians far removed from the events they depicted. Scholarship has advanced considerably since von Rad's *Holy War,* but virtually all of the issues he addressed remain topics of debate. And the debate begins with the text here offered to English readers.

---

97. Pp. 46-54. Lind's views on Israel's theology of warfare and on the politics associated with it are collected in *Monotheism, Power, Justice: Collected Old Testament Essays.* Text Reader Series 3 (Elkhart: Institute of Mennonite Studies, 1990). Cf. Kang, 114-125.

Holy War
in Ancient Israel

Editor's Preface

ALTHOUGH GERHARD VON RAD's book, *Der heilige Krieg im alten Israel,* is very old and greatly challenged, it has been the basis for all subsequent work on the subject of holy war. Attempts at modernizing often reflect contemporary psychological underpinnings and seem to miss von Rad's intentions. Consequently, we have aimed in this translation for precise but readable duplication of his wording and have tried to reproduce his thought as accurately as possible and yet in accessible language.

In the places where there are clerical errors in the German original (such as citation errors in the footnotes, mistaken identification of the biblical speaker in quotations, and misnumbering of biblical verses), these have been corrected when the mistakes are obvious and when the bibliographical materials have been found. Great gratitude is due to Ed Conrad for his correcting and completing of von Rad's very minimal footnotes.

This project would not have been possible without John H. Yoder's foundational help with the first reading of the German text, and we thank him for envisioning this joint project with Ben Ollenburger's and Judith Sanderson's contributions. Finally, special thanks must also be given to Herold C. Gersmehl for his invaluable assistance in comparing the original German text with the final revisions of the English translation.

Introduction

WORK ON THE OLD TESTAMENT today is largely determined by the
question of institutions. The form-critical research initiated by
Hermann Gunkel has led to sharp distinctions between quite
diverse *Sitze im Leben*. These *Sitze im Leben*—each of them a
focal point of public, sacral, or judicial life—are seen as the places
in which tradition, formed according to precise rules, was preserved. For the functioning of these institutions, to the ordering of
which everyone willingly submitted, was thinkable for the ancients
only if behind them stood the obligating power of a long tradition,
and only if at the very beginning Yahweh himself had put them in
place. Therefore, the royal court, the cult, and the judicial life—
to name only the most general institutions—were the preservers
of quite definite traditions, whose conservative capacity to endure
we Occidentals, who have become both formally and substantially
traditionless, can hardly overestimate.

It is clear from this perspective that the concept of the "religion
of the people of Israel" must be greatly revised. Did there ever
exist such a thing as that complex of religious ideas about God
and creation, the person, sin and forgiveness, and so forth hovering
over the people of Israel like a spiritual cloud? In the oldest times
certainly not. We take this conviction so far that whenever we do
find some conception of faith living freely in the people we first
ask for its *Sitz im Leben* and for the institutions from which it
might have issued or by which it could have been supported. That
is methodologically quite proper.

39

Although this branch of investigation has already progressed to quite detailed insights, research has hitherto ignored, or at least neglected to define and to pursue, the particular stream of traditions borne by one of the sacral institutions of ancient Israel—namely, holy war. The proof that in holy war we are dealing with a sacral institution in the full sense of the word could easily be uncovered—if that would at all be necessary. More difficult is the question of method, how we can grasp the widely-scattered material properly and gain entry into the questions it raises. Any attempt to begin simply from the most ancient holy wars which are reported historically would fail; we know that there is doubt as to whether the dominant picture of the holy wars in the tradition available to us corresponds to historical reality in the time of the Conquest. Even if we did encounter one or two reliable reports, it would hardly afford us a basis broad enough to bear the weight of investigation. We have, therefore, no other path than first of all to project quite rigorously a theory of holy war with the help of the rich, and certainly mostly old, traditional materials contained within the narratives. The general picture thus gained must then be subjected to criticism through historical, literary-historical, and theological evaluation.

CHAPTER 1

The Theory of Holy War

MUSTERING FOR A HOLY WAR took place by means of a *blast of the trumpet.*

> [Gideon] sounded the trumpet, and the Abiezrites were called out (זָעַק) to follow him. And he sent messengers throughout all Manasseh; and they too were called out to follow him. And he sent messengers to Asher, Zebulun, and Naphtali; and they went up to meet them. (Judg. 6:34-35; cf. 3:27; 1 Sam. 13:3)

An especially ancient form was the sending out of pieces of sacrificial flesh by messengers.[1] This was done in order to compel participation in the enterprise. Willingness for military service could hardly be taken for granted.[2] The external and internal cost demanded of the individual (one thinks of the extreme cultic demands) was very high. The Song of Deborah expresses amazement about the people's willingness (הִתְנַדֵּב) and praises it twice (Judg. 5:2, 9). Then the troops streamed together (vv. 14-15).

Once the army had gathered in the camp it was called *"the people of Yahweh"* (עַם יהוה or עַם הָאֱלֹהִים) (Judg. 5:11, 13; 20:2). The term generally means, of course, the amphictyonic mustering of all the men, but especially when such a gathering is done for

---

1. Wilhelm Caspari, "Was stand im Buch der Kriege Jahwes?" *ZWT* 54 (1912): 141. Martin Noth, *Das System der zwölf Stämme Israels.* BWANT 52 [4/1] (1930; repr. Stuttgart: Kohlhammer, 1966).
2. Kurt Möhlenbrink, "Sauls Ammoniterfeldzug und Samuels Beitrag zum Königtum des Saul," *ZAW* 58 (1940/41): 59 n. 2.

the purpose of war (cf. 2 Sam. 1:12).[3] The designation צְבָאוֹת יהוה
(Exod. 12:41) in the priestly tradition is distinctive; in another case
it is מַעַרְכוֹת אֱלֹהִים (1 Sam. 17:26).

Henceforth the army stood under severe sacral regulations.
The *men were "consecrated"* (קדשׁ; Josh. 3:5). They submitted
to sexual renunciation (1 Sam. 21:5; 2 Sam. 11:11-12). Certainly
the making of vows also played a role (Num. 21:2; Judg. 11:36;
1 Sam. 14:24). The entire camp community had to be ritually pure
(Deut. 23:9-14) because Yahweh was present in the camp (אֱלֹהֶיךָ
מִתְהַלֵּךְ בְּקֶרֶב מַחֲנֶךָ וִיהוה). Also, the weapons were consecrated
(1 Sam. 21:5; 2 Sam. 1:21).

If the occasion for the mustering was a misfortune suffered
under enemy attack, the entire army underwent a ceremony of
repentance and mourning (Judg. 20:23, 26; 1 Sam. 30:4; 11:4).

With an eye on the coming battle, the army *offered sacrifices*
(1 Sam. 7:9; 13:9-10, 12). Especially important was the *oracle of
God* (Judg. 20:13, 18; 1 Sam. 7:9; 14:8ff. [here the obtaining of a
sign from God is already secularized]; 14:37; 23:2, 4, 9-12; 28:6;
30:7-8; 2 Sam. 5:19, 23).[4]

On the basis of an affirmative divine decision, the leader
proclaimed to the militia: *"Yahweh has given the . . . into our
hand."* This cry is certainly to be understood in the perfect and
not as a future. It may sometimes have already been a part of the
message carried by the herald who summoned the militia; at the
latest it would have taken place immediately before the battle.

> Josh. 2:24 (report of the spies): "Truly the LORD has given all
> the land into our hands."
>
> Josh. 6:2 (Yahweh speaking to Joshua): "See, I have given
> into your hand Jericho . . ."

3. Leonhard Rost, "Die Bezeichnungen für Land und Volk im alten Israel,"
Festschrift Otto Procksch, ed. Albrecht Alt (Leipzig: J. C. Hinrichs and A. Deichert, 1934), 145-46.

4. Richard Press, "Das Ordal im alten Israel II," *ZAW* 51 (1933): 231-35.

Josh. 6:16 (Joshua to the people): "Shout; for the LORD has given you the city."

Josh. 8:1 (Yahweh to Joshua): "See, I have given into your hand the king of Ai . . ."

Josh. 8:18 (Yahweh to Joshua): "Stretch out the javelin . . . for I will give it [Ai] (אֶתְּנֶנָּה) into your hand."

Josh. 10:8 (Yahweh to Joshua): ". . . for I have given them into your hands."

Josh. 10:19 (Joshua to the army): ". . . for the LORD your God has given them into your hand."

Judg. 3:28 (Ehud to the army): "the LORD has given your enemies . . . into your hand."

Judg. 4:7 (Yahweh to Barak): ". . . and I will give him [Sisera] into your hand."

Judg. 4:14 (Deborah to Barak): ". . . this is the day in which the LORD has given Sisera into your hand."

Judg. 7:9 (Yahweh to Gideon): "Arise, . . . for I have given it [the camp] into your hand."

Judg. 7:15 (Gideon to his people): "Arise; for the LORD has given the host of Midian into your hand."

Judg. 18:10 (spies to the Danites): "God has given it [Philistia] into your hands."

Judg. 20:28 (Yahweh to Israel): "tomorrow I will give them [the Benjaminites] into your hand."

1 Sam. 14:12 (Jonathan to his armor-bearer): "the LORD has given them [the Philistines] into the hand of Israel."

1 Sam. 17:46 (David to Goliath): "This day the LORD will deliver you (יְסַגֶּרְךָ) into my hand."

1 Sam. 23:4 (Yahweh to David): ". . . for I will give the Philistines into your hand."

1 Sam. 24:4 (Yahweh to David): "Behold, I will give your enemy into your hand."

1 Sam. 26:8 (Abishai to David): "God has given (סִגַּר) your enemy into your hand this day."

1 Kgs. 20:28 (Yahweh to Ahab): ". . . I will give all this great multitude into your hand."

This listing makes evident that the phrase is rooted in the phenomenon of holy war and at the same time demonstrates its importance. Its form as direct address by Yahweh is surely primary over against the version in the third person, for the sentence is derived from a direct divine oracle, which may be one of the most important factors in the entire phenomenon of holy war. On this oracle was based the utterly unshakeable certainty of victory, which was the characteristic defining all holy war.[5]

Now the militia marched toward the enemy. *Yahweh moved out ahead of them* (יהוה יָצָא לְפְנֵי or הָלַךְ עִם; Judg. 4:14; Deut. 20:4; similarly 2 Sam. 5:24). According to Josh. 3:11 the ark of Yahweh preceded (עָבַר) Israel.

Before the battle the troops readied themselves "before Yahweh" (חָלַץ לִפְנֵי יהוה) (Num. 32:20ff., 27, 29, 32; Josh. 4:13). But the preparation and the arming and especially the number of the warriors were not of decisive significance (Judg. 7:2ff.; 1 Sam. 14:6; 17:45, 47). One would be ashamed to count the army, because what is a miracle should not be rationalized (2 Sam. 24:1ff.; cf. Exod. 30:12 [P]).

These wars are *Yahweh's wars* (מִלְחֲמוֹת יהוה; 1 Sam. 18:17; 25:28; cf. Num. 21:14). The enemies are *Yahweh's enemies* (אֹיְבֵי יהוה; Judg. 5:31; 1 Sam. 30:26). The one who acts is Yahweh alone.

Exod. 14:4: " . . . I [Yahweh] will . . . get glory over Pharaoh."
Exod. 14:14: "The LORD will fight for you."
Exod. 14:18: " . . . shall know that I am the LORD, when I have gotten glory over Pharaoh."

5. Johannes P. E. Pedersen, *Israel, Its Life and Culture,* 3 (1940; repr. London: Oxford University Press, 1963), 15 ("perfect certainty of victory").

Deut. 1:30: "The LORD your God who goes before you will himself fight for you."

Josh. 10:14: . . . for the LORD fought for Israel.

Josh. 10:42: . . . because the LORD God of Israel fought for Israel.

Josh. 11:6: " . . . for tomorrow at this time I will give over all of them, slain, to Israel."

Josh. 23:10: " . . . since it is the LORD your God who fights for you."

Judg. 20:35: And the LORD defeated Benjamin before Israel.

1 Sam. 14:23: So the LORD delivered Israel that day (cf. v. 39).

This activity of Yahweh is what determines—in a psychological respect, first of all—the behavior of Israel as well as that of the enemies. *Israel must not fear but must believe.*

Exod. 14:13-14 (Moses to Israel): "Fear not, stand firm, and see the salvation of the LORD . . . you have only to be still."

Deut. 20:3 (priest to the army): "Let not your heart faint; do not fear."

Josh. 8:1 (Yahweh to Joshua): "Do not fear or be dismayed."

Josh. 10:8 (Yahweh to Joshua): "Do not fear them."

Josh. 10:25 (Joshua to the people): "Do not be afraid or dismayed; be strong and of good courage."

Josh. 11:6 (Yahweh to Joshua): "Do not be afraid of them."

Judg. 7:3 (Gideon to the army): "Whoever is fearful and trembling, let him return home."

1 Sam. 23:16-17: Jonathan . . . strengthened his [David's] hand in God. And he said to him, "Fear not."

1 Sam. 30:6: But David strengthened himself in the LORD his God.

2 Sam. 10:12 (Joab to David): "Be of good courage, and let us play the man for our people . . . and may the LORD do what seems good to him."

It could be objected that this list contains essentially only
Deuteronomic material and thereby shows only how the older traditions had been reworked by a relatively later, literary style. Nonetheless, there can be no doubt that a word of encouragement and a
call to faith in Yahweh must have had an important function in the
ancient holy wars as well. The warriors had to be acceptable to
Yahweh in every respect and had to be bearers of Yahweh's intention even with regard to their inner disposition. Thus, for example,
the removal of the weak and fearful (Judg. 7:3ff.), because they
constituted a danger for the enterprise, strikes us as very ancient.
We must speak further of the fact that this entire motif was later
sublimated and theologized in a very reflective way.

The other impact of the fact that Yahweh acts alone concerns
the enemy: *The enemy loses courage.*

> Exod. 15:14-16 (Moses and people to Yahweh):
> "The peoples have heard, they tremble;
>> pangs have seized on the inhabitants of Philistia.
> Now are the chiefs of Edom dismayed;
>> the leaders of Moab, trembling seizes them;
>> all the inhabitants of Canaan have melted away.
> Terror and dread fall upon them;
>> . . . they are as still as a stone."
> Exod. 23:27-28 (Yahweh to Israel): "I will send my terror
> (אֵימָתִי) before you, and . . . I will send discouragement[6]
> (צִרְעָה) before you."
> Deut. 2:25 (Yahweh to the people): "I will begin to put the
> dread and fear of you upon the peoples . . . [so they] shall
> tremble and be in anguish because of you."
> Deut. 11:25 (Moses to Israel): "The LORD your God will

---

6. צִרְעָה = "Niedergeschlagenheit"; Ludwig Köhler, "Hebräische Vokabeln
I," *ZAW* 54 (1936): 291. [Trans. note: Von Rad here and in Josh. 24:12 accepts
the interpretation that the word "hornet" should be understood not literally but as
an image for *Entmutigung* or "discouragement."]

lay the fear of you and the dread of you upon all the
land."

Josh. 2:9 (Rahab to the spies): "The fear of you has fallen
upon us, and . . . all the inhabitants of the land melt away
before you."

Josh. 2:24 (spies to Joshua): "All the inhabitants of the land
are fainthearted (נָמֹגוּ) because of us."

Josh. 5:1: Their heart [the Canaanites'] melted (וַיִּמַּס), and
there was no longer any spirit (רוּחַ) in them, because of
the people of Israel.

Josh. 10:2: . . . he [Adonizedek, king of Jerusalem] feared
greatly.

Josh. 11:20: For it was the LORD's doing to harden their [the
Gibeonites'] hearts that they should come against Israel
in battle.

Josh. 24:12 (Yahweh to Israel): "I sent the discouragement
[see Exod. 23:27-28 above] before you."

1 Sam. 4:7-8: The Philistines were afraid; for they said, . . .
"Woe to us! . . . Woe to us! Who can deliver us from the
power of these mighty gods?"

At this point we must refer as well to the setbacks experienced
in holy wars; Israel's failures must be named.

Lev. 26:36: "And . . . I will send faintness (מֹרֶךְ) into their
hearts . . . ; the sound of a driven leaf shall put them to
flight."

Josh. 7:5: And the hearts of the people melted, and became
as water.

1 Sam. 17:11: . . . they [Israelites] were dismayed and greatly
afraid.

1 Sam. 28:5: He [Saul] was afraid, and his heart trembled
greatly.

The battle itself opened with a *war cry* (תְּרוּעָה). One such battle cry is preserved for us in Judg. 7:20 (cf. Josh. 6:5; 1 Sam. 17:20, 52).[7] Later we will encounter this element again (2 Chr. 20:21-22) in an extremely spiritualized form.[8]

The outward circumstances under which the battles took place were naturally extremely diverse. This makes all the more striking the uniformity with which the narrators describe Yahweh's intervention. It is a matter of the *divine terror* which comes over the enemy.

Exod. 23:27: "I . . . will throw into confusion (המם) all the people against whom you shall come."

Deut. 7:23: "But the LORD your God will . . . throw them into [a] great [devastating] confusion (הָמָם מְהוּמָה)."

Josh. 10:10: And the LORD threw them into a panic (המם) before Israel.

Josh. 10:11: . . . the LORD threw down great stones from heaven upon them.

Josh. 24:7: " . . . he [the LORD] put darkness between you and the Egyptians."

Judg. 4:15: And the LORD [brought] Sisera and all his chariots [into confusion] (המם).

Judg. 7:22: . . . the LORD set every man's sword against his fellow and against all the army.

1 Sam. 5:11: For there was a deathly panic (מְהוּמַת־מָוֶת) throughout the whole city. The hand of God was very heavy there.

1 Sam. 7:10: But the LORD thundered with a mighty voice that day against the Philistines and threw them into confusion.

1 Sam. 14:15: And there was a panic (חֲרָדָה) in the camp . . . the earth quaked; and it became a very great panic (חֶרְדַּת אֱלֹהִים [divine terror]).

7. Caspari, 146-47. Paul Humbert, *La "Terou'a": Analyse d'un rite biblique* (Neuchâtel: Secrétariat de l'Université, 1946), 29. Cf. also Exod. 17:16.
8. Cf. below, 129-131.

> 1 Sam. 14:20: . . . and behold, every man's sword was against his fellow, and there was very great confusion (מְהוּמָה).

This overview makes clear that Yahweh's intervention in the form of a confusing divine terror was an indispensable element of the tradition.[9] What happened was that, in the panic created by Yahweh, the battle order of the enemy and often also the camp came into such confusion that sometimes the enemies destroyed each other. Without question it was the intention of the narrator to attribute the causation of victory to Yahweh alone, yet in no way did that exclude belligerent activity on the part of Israel. Taking part in such a battle is occasionally referred to uninhibitedly as "coming to help Yahweh" (Judg. 5:23). In the earliest times there were no intellectual problems involved in the concept of such synergism, even though the act which was decisive was that of Yahweh.[10] The later rise of theological reflection was to reduce the cooperation of Israel and diminish its importance to that of some kind of demonstration (Judg. 7:16ff.).

The highpoint and the conclusion of the holy war is formed by the *ḥērem,* the consecration of the booty to Yahweh. As is the case for the entire holy war, this too is a cultic phenomenon: human beings and animals are slaughtered, gold and silver and the like go as קֹדֶשׁ into Yahweh's treasury (Josh. 6:18-19).[11] However, as this entire procedure of battle—although sacrally prescribed— also had about it something very strongly improvised, so the im-

---

9. In a doom oracle Israel also stands under the threat of such a divine terror: "They [Israel] shall stumble over one another, as if to escape a sword, though none pursues" (Lev. 26:37).

10. Cf. perhaps Josh. 11:6: "I [Yahweh] will give over all of them, slain, to Israel." Then in v. 8: "And the LORD gave them into the hand of Israel . . . and they smote them."

11. This same practice will be portrayed by the Mesha Stela (Moabite Stone) as "satiation (intoxication) for Chemosh"; trans. William F. Albright, in *Ancient Near Eastern Texts,* ed. James B. Pritchard, 3rd ed. (Princeton: Princeton University Press, 1969), 320.

plementation of this rite exhibits considerable differences.[12] It is not useful to pursue these variations here; they do not raise any problem, especially when one considers the fact that here— namely, in the literary description—the theory of the narrator could readily play to such a special degree as to bring about exaggeration. Whether historically there was an evolution in the sense of a progressive mitigation and humanization is at least questionable in the light of the radical perspective of the Deuteronomist. That carrying out the *ḥērem* could be regarded as a *status confessionis* (1 Sam. 15)—that is, that some other possible way to behave even came into question—can only be understood as the sign of a development already quite far along and even approaching a crisis, which we shall have to describe yet more fully. Likewise the conception of *ḥērem* as a vow (Num. 21:2) must be more recent than that which understands it as executing a command of Yahweh (1 Sam. 15:3) because a pledge already presupposes a decision about whether to carry it out or to renounce it. On the purely terminological level, the texts with their stereotyped use of the concept of חֵרֶם do not show us anything particular.[13]

The end of the holy war was then the dismissal of the militia with the cry, *"To your tents, O Israel!"* In direct discourse this cry has been preserved for us only in 2 Sam. 20:1 and 1 Kgs. 12:16 (cf. 1 Kgs. 22:36). But more frequent is the stereotyped perfect-tense report that each went (or fled) to his tent, which precisely signifies the dismissal of the militia and the end of the enterprise (1 Sam. 4:10; 2 Sam. 18:17; 19:8; 20:22; 2 Kgs. 8:21; 14:12; cf. Judg. 20:8).

---

12. Of the dissimilarity between the conception and the execution—especially with regard to the extent of the decline of the *ḥērem*—we can easily make ourselves a picture (Num. 21:2; Deut. 2:34ff.; 3:6ff.; 7:1ff.; 7:26; 20:13ff.; Josh. 6:21; 8:26; 10:28; 11:11-12; 1 Sam. 15:3; 30:26; 2 Sam. 8:11; 1 Kgs. 7:51; 15:15; 2 Kgs. 12:18).

13. Concerning the correlation of the reflections of the remnant with the practice of "absolute wars," see Werner E. Müller, *Die Vorstellung vom Rest im Alten Testament* (Leipzig: Hoppe, 1939), 18-21; new edition by Horst Dietrich Preuss (Neukirchen-Vluyn: Neukirchener, 1973), 26-29.

Thus, we can indeed consider holy war as an eminently cultic undertaking—that is, prescribed and sanctioned by fixed, traditional, sacred rites and observances. "The armed camp, the cradle of the nation, was also its most ancient holy of holies. There was Israel and there was Yahweh."[14]

14. Julius Wellhausen, *Israelitische und jüdische Geschichte,* 3rd ed. (Berlin: Georg Reimer, 1897), 26.

CHAPTER 2

Holy War in the History
of Ancient Israel

EVEN THOUGH THE COMPOSITE PICTURE of the elements of tradition which we have set forth has been drawn from sources of the greatest variety, it cannot be said that we have made an arbitrary collection of heterogeneous material. On the contrary, one sees here already in outline a cultic celebration of considerable historical credibility. Nonetheless, we must note: hardly could such a holy war ever have been carried out in such orthodox and schematic completeness. If we move into the realm of actual history, this rigidity will quickly be eliminated. In fact, certainly never did one holy war resemble another. Rather, each one was somewhat unique in the way it was carried out, including within itself such a fullness of surprises and wonders that the observer can certainly not be too cautious about any homogenization or generalization, to which we ourselves are naturally inclined.

I

Therefore, according to proper method, we ask first the question of the actual historical *Sitz im Leben* which this cultic institution must unquestionably have had at one time in ancient Israel. The answer which the relevant narrative literature, first of all, suggests with overwhelming unanimity directs us to the time of the immigration and the Conquest. However, the idea that Israel moved through the desert in a great phalanx and then seized the land of Palestine has step by step been eliminated by recent research as utterly schematic and theoretical. The first blow was struck by literary criticism; it became apparent that this generalizing idea had developed through the skillful composition of many individual sagas and that beside this composition or in it other traditions are visible, according to which the tribes took over their particular territories in the arable land one at a time and independently. For instance, in Judg. 1 in the framework of ancient lists a conception is expressed which is very much older than the generalizing portrayal of the book of Joshua. And as far as this is concerned, it contains within its narrative component traditions which in fact describe the conquest of the land of just one tribe, namely Benjamin.[1] All of that has long been recognized, so that our question could only be this: did the tribes, operating individually, take over their territories through the process of the sacral form of holy war? In the case of Benjamin, the conception of a military conquest— to name only the best known example—has already undergone thorough revision, as a result of archaeological findings with regard to the famous seizure of the city of Ai (Josh. 7–8). Excavations have demonstrated with certainty that Ai was abandoned already in the Early Bronze Age and was first resettled only in the early Israelite era.[2] Thus a military conquest by Israel could not have taken place here. In the yet more famous collapse of Jericho (Josh. 6) the situation is not very different. In any case, it would be difficult to connect the destruction of the great walls, which had already taken place in the 15th century, with the immigration of

---

1. Albrecht Alt, "Josua," *Werden und Wesen des Alten Testaments,* ed. Paul Volz, Friedrich Stummer, and Johannes Hempel. BZAW 66 (1936): 13-29; repr. *Kleine Schriften zur Geschichte des Volkes Israel,* 1 (Munich: C. H. Beck, 1953): 176-192.
    2. Martin Noth, "Bethel und Ai," *PJ* 31 (1935): 14-15; repr. *Aufsätze zur biblischen Landes- und Altertumskunde* (Neukirchen-Vluyn: Neukirchener, 1971), 1:216.

Benjamin. An additional unfavorable factor to weigh is that the etiological *Tendenz* concerning the walls represents a more recent stratum of the narrative of Josh. 6 and betrays the relatively late chronological position of its narrator.[3]

Nevertheless, the oldest account in Judg. 1 (J) does support the picture of a military action:

> After the death of Joshua the people of Israel inquired of the LORD, "Who shall go up first for us against the Canaanites, to fight against them?" The LORD said, "Judah shall go up . . ." And Judah said to Simeon his brother, "Come up with me into the territory allotted to me, that we may fight against the Canaanites. . . ." (Judg. 1:1-3a)

But even this conception cannot correspond to actual historical reality. In several penetrating studies Albrecht Alt has taught us to see the progress of the Conquest by the tribes in a way which is certainly very much nearer to historical reality.[4] First we must consider that the region of settlement of the Israelite tribes was largely the yet uncultivated Palestinian hill country; only in a considerably later phase of its history did Israel push into the plains with their system of old Canaanite city-states. That consideration itself indicates that the probability of a military clash would not have been very great. So also the progress of the Conquest itself now appears to us in another light: the shepherd nomads who through all of history have been infiltrating the arable land from the desert were utterly unprepared militarily. Indeed, at first, in the pattern of changing pastures they sojourned there only in the summer and then in the rainy season returned to the steppes, which again would provide them with sustenance. So must the Israelite tribes have arranged it as well, and in this phase of the development their relationship with the cities—if they came into contact with

---

3. Martin Noth, *Das Buch Josua,* 2nd ed. HAT 7 (Tübingen: J. C. B. Mohr, 1953): 21.

4. Albrecht Alt, "Erwägungen über die Landnahme der Israeliten in Palästina," *PJ* 35 (1939): 8-63; repr. *Kleine Schriften,* 1:126-175.

them at all—was predominantly that of friendly negotiation.[5] But now it is clear that the general weakening of the political sovereignty which Egypt had exercised must have gradually invited these nomads to cease their wandering to and fro and to remain permanently. But even then as a rule there still would not yet have been military clashes, since already the cities among the hills (as Alt has shown) were always created only on the fringes of the settlement area of these tribes. It thus becomes clear that the real military clashes with the Canaanites were secondary to the actual Conquest.[6]

That of course should not mean that there could not be any wars at all in the time of the Conquest or even earlier. But if we have first of all freed ourselves from the powerful suggestion of the book of Joshua concerning the historical reality, then almost all tangible material quickly disappears with which we could actually fix historically such military events as did no doubt happen here or there. Even in what concerns the time before the Conquest we must be very careful about dealing with particular tribes as if they were important figures that remain constant. Tribes die off, merge into one another, and so forth. And if it might actually be the case that tribes at first adopted for themselves the names of the Palestinian regions, that also admonishes us to be cautious.[7] First, we could attribute holy wars to the Joseph group, which came from the Reed Sea and brought to Palestine faith in Yahweh. But the battle against the Amalekites in the far south near Kadesh, recounted in Exod. 17:8ff., also seems to fall into a very early

5. The narrators of Gen. 26 and 34 give us a picture of such relationships.

6. "It is in principle unlikely that a people coming out of a nomadic lifestyle could have elevated the militant side of their God to the middle point of their life. . . . In fact, as it can be shown, the Israelites were drawn into a military reality without being asked whether they agreed to it. They underwent painful education for war under foreign teachers who were not seeking their well-being, and thereby they learned eventually to stand up for themselves honorably" (Caspari, "Was stand im Buch der Kriege Jahwes?" 110-11).

7. That has been suggested for Ephraim and Judah in Martin Noth, *The Old Testament World* (Philadelphia: Fortress, 1966), 55-58.

time. In this case we would have to think perhaps of the alliance of the Leah group (Reuben, Simeon, Levi, Judah, Issachar, Zebulun) or, better, of parts thereof.[8] That these tribes were already bonded together in an amphictyonic covenant, certainly chronologically before the formation of the twelve-tribe amphictyony, is probable. But what do we know of their worship? So here also we have only the probability that in a very early time something more or less like a holy war was carried on, since the narrator has fashioned the history completely from the later perspective of the Israelite amphictyony. To want to enter into a description of what a holy war might be without knowing something of its cultic background would be absurd. And that is true of all such vestiges of tradition.[9]

II

If we would take our point of departure uncritically from the picture that the book of Judges in its present form gives us, then our findings with regard to how Israel waged war would be about the same as for the times of the Conquest and the desert wanderings: Israel fought its enemies in holy war with miraculous unanimity and uniformity. The historical situation of this epoch, however, must from the outset be judged differently. The Israel (in the form of the twelve-tribe amphictyony) about which the Hexateuch sources constantly speak, while they generalize after the fact from particular traditions, had now arrived on the scene of history. Thus we come, from a historical perspective, to incomparably more solid ground. Further, one must remember in connection with the old histories of the judges — if one can only

8. However, cf. Martin Noth, *A History of Pentateuchal Traditions* (1972; repr. Atlanta: Scholars Press, 1989), 50.

9. Our guesses would be just as vague if we were to attempt to draw into the picture the battles of the Calebites and Kenizzites (Josh. 10:28ff.) to which Karl Elliger has pointed in "Josua in Judäa," *PJ* 30 (1934): 70.

disengage them from their generalizing, dogmatizing Deuteronomistic surroundings—that the distance in time between the
reports and the historical events of which they speak is very much
shorter; by contrast, in the case of the miracle of the Sea or the
wars in the desert period that distance is hundreds of years.

We take our point of departure from the most striking event
of this epoch, the battle of Deborah. We scarcely need to say a
word to show that the song in Judg. 5 understands the event as a
holy war: the praise of Yahweh, who made the soldiers into a
unified and willing army (vv. 2, 9); Yahweh's personal coming to
the battle; his intervening from heaven; curse and blessing—all
of that shows that the event took place throughout as in a sacral
space and in sacral forms. One must only consider that the song
itself is no longer a real cult hymn and that as a victory song it is
no longer exclusively interested in the narrowest cultic frame of
reference. To expect a complete portrayal of the rituals of these
holy wars from the song would be just as unreasonable as to ask
about its failure to mention the full listing of the tribes that were
present. The fact that the prose account (Judg. 4) coincides essentially with the data of the song stirs a favorable prejudgment with
regard to it, as well as for the similar accounts which we must still
consult. When the prose text deviates from the data of the song in
small details, no one who knows how historical traditions work
would be surprised. The opposite would be much more suspect.[10]

The relatedness of the two texts is probably not to be explained
as simply literary in the sense of a literary derivation of one text
from the other,[11] nor is it to be easily understood as the history

10. I do not consider it as a difference that the prose text mentions Jabin of
Hazor, who now comes into the account as the actual head of the enemy coalition
above Sisera. That is to be judged not as a deviation of the same tradition but
rather as a secondary and only literary mixing. What is truly bothersome with the
tradition of Josh. 11:1ff. is only the difference concerning the tribes which were
involved. The song names six; Judg. 4, only Zebulon and Naphtali. Cf. also Ernst
Sellin, "Zu Jud. 5$_{15a\beta}$," ZAW 59 (1942/43): 218.

11. According to Otto Eissfeldt, the "Sisera recension" is dependent upon
the song. *Die Quellen des Richterbuches in Synoptischer Anordnung ins Deutsche*

which is behind both of the texts. Rather, the connection rests much more on the oral tradition lying between both entities. That such an oral tradition both arises rapidly and then also quickly takes on a certain fixed form (i.e., that a certain "myth formation" tends to begin almost immediately after an event) is richly documented from old and new examples. As a whole, the prose is somewhat more secular than the song in its conception of the event. Nonetheless, in a very small space Judg. 4:14-16 portrays in almost gap-free completeness the constitutive foundational elements of what is almost a small prototype of a holy war:

> And Deborah said to Barak, "Up! For this is the day in which the LORD has given Sisera into your hand. Does not the LORD go out before you?" So Barak went down from Mount Tabor with ten thousand men following him. And the LORD routed Sisera and all his chariots and all his army before Barak at the edge of the sword; and Sisera alighted from his chariot and fled away on foot. And Barak pursued the chariots and the army to Harosheth-ha-goiim, and all the army of Sisera fell by the edge of the sword; not a man was left.

Here we can with assurance now grasp a holy war historically; for no one will claim that the song and the prose account, with their sacral pictures of the event, had first given the event a meaning which would have been foreign to the immediate bearers of that event. Constitutive for the event is the collective behavior of the tribes, which in this epoch were living manifestly in isolation and without closer political bonding to a comprehensive political whole. Even if not in perfect completeness, still there arose in this battle "Israel," and not merely one tribe or a group of tribes. Israel felt itself obligated to follow the call and the leadership of the charismatic leader, and Yahweh gave the victory. The battle of Deborah was hardly the first undertaking in such a high sacral

---

Übersetzt samt einer in Einleitung und Noten Gegebenen Begründung (Leipzig: J. C. Hinrichs, 1925), 31.

style. But the song, in its marveling at the event, declares something important: in this event the tribes experienced themselves as "Israel"—that is, as a unity led and protected by Yahweh. More accurately, they unexpectedly experienced that their cultic bond with Yahweh also had far-reaching consequences on the political level. At that time Israel began to be a people.

Here we immediately add a brief description of the event which, together with all of the results it produced, concluded the epoch of the judges—namely, Saul's war against the Ammonites (1 Sam. 11). The enemy here is one of the eastern peoples which seriously threatens one of the exposed outposts of Israel, the city Jabesh in Gilead. Kurt Möhlenbrink has shown that the political scope of this attack on the east Jordan city went essentially farther than this merely anecdotal account directly articulates.[12] But even if the intention of Ammon was not exactly a liquidation of the entire covenant of tribes as a political factor, still the threat was very grave in conjunction with the threat of the Philistines on the west side. Here again the call to arms is proclaimed by a charismatic leader. Unfortunately, the number of the participating tribes can be estimated only by means of very uncertain inference, for the reference in 1 Sam. 11:8 to "Israel" and "Judah" is surely a coarse anachronism.[13] In other ways as well the story carries a good many signs of the later standpoint of its narrator, not least in the way in which the portrayal has already been secularized. It pays its respects to the old sacral ideas only in the majestic report of Saul's summons (vv. 6-7) and in the closing word of Samuel about the saving act of Yahweh. But precisely because the narrator brings these features to the account, almost like something that had become foreign to him, we have no reason to doubt the previously much more sacral form in which this war was actually

---

12. "Sauls Ammoniterfeldzug," 57-70.
13. Möhlenbrink thinks of Benjamin, Reuben, and Gad (p. 62). Noth adds also Ephraim and Manasseh; "Das Land Gilead als Siedlungsgebiet israelitischer Sippen," *PJ* 37 (1941): 82 n. 1; repr. *Aufsätze zur biblischen Landes- und Altertumskunde,* 1:374 n. 81.

carried out. How strongly the entire body of Israel felt itself endangered by the threat to the outpost of Jabesh could not be demonstrated more precisely than through the fact that an unknown person in the tribe of Benjamin, far from the threatened point, was raised up as leader of the relief campaign. Precisely this logic of the event is the best proof that in Saul the amphictyony arose— that is, that it was a holy war. There is thus no doubt that still in the time of Saul Israel's wars were conducted as holy wars. In this connection the story of Saul's victory over the Philistines (1 Sam. 14) gives an especially coherent picture. The preceding skirmish had already taken place under mysterious concomitants: the earth shook, and a divine terror brought disorder into the enemy camp (1 Sam. 14:15). Especially explicit, however, are the events during the playing out of the battle itself: the questioning of God (v. 18), the vows of continence (v. 24), the numinous panic which made the enemies kill one another (v. 20), the sacrifice and the building of an altar (vv. 33-35).[14]

With these two events, the battle of Deborah and the uprising of Israel under Saul—both represented for us by credible traditions and to some extent within the realm of accessible history—the space in time during which Israel fought holy wars is approximately marked out. The literary source materials for this time (namely, the histories of the judges in their pre-Deuteronomistic redactional form) have an admittedly strongly anecdotal character; still they give us all kinds of credible material, which we can consult without hesitation to ascertain the old events.

The story of Ehud-Eglon (Judg. 3:12-30) leads us into very old times because Moab is still presupposed as Jericho's opposite-side neighbor.[15] It was not until later that Reuben and Gad first pushed into that east Jordan territory which had previously been

---

14. Concerning Saul's "War against the Amalekites" in 1 Sam. 15, see 94ff. below.

15. Martin Noth, "Israelitische Stämme zwischen Ammon und Moab," ZAW 60 (1944): 17-19; repr. Aufsätze zur biblischen Landes- und Altertumskunde, 1:397-99.

Moabite. Only Eglon's attack over the Jordan against Jericho, therefore, and not his existence on the other side of the Jordan in the "fields of Moab," is considered unacceptable to Israel. This time the tribe under immediate attack is itself the bearer of the defense enterprise. Ehud, a member of the Benjamite delegation which was responsible to carry the tribute to the enemy king, kills Eglon (obviously in Jericho itself)[16] and then sounds the trumpet on the mountains of Ephraim. We know nothing more precise about the extent of those involved in the war or of the contingent summoned by Ehud. But it is characteristic of the amphictyonic sense of belonging together that Ehud could very naturally claim the assistance also of more remote tribes (or at least those not immediately victimized), and indeed he does receive it.

It has long been known that in the story of Gideon's war against the Midianites (Judg. 7:1ff.) two quite distinct narratives have been coupled together into a unity. According to one part of the account (Judg. 7:1–8:3), the heads of the enemies are called Oreb and Zeeb; according to the other account (8:4-21), Zebah and Zalmunna. This distinguishing of the narrative material is important for our concern, for only the first account reveals clearly that the enterprise is one of those holy wars. The fact that around the time of the harvest the rapacious Midianites, camel nomads from the northern Arabian desert who came apparently over the land east of Jordan, could flood over Palestine all the way to the Philistine plain shows the high degree of weakness into which the covenant of tribes had fallen. This time it is a Manassite who gives the signal for the uprising. Unfortunately again, this saga is not entirely clear about the size of the contingent. According to Judg. 6:35, Manasseh, along with Asher and Zebulon [and Naphtali], provided military service. This is the army, however, that was then reduced by Gideon to three hundred men. So we may assume that Gideon's contingent was very small, all the more so since the saga speaks first of the participation of Naphtali, Asher, Manasseh, and

16. Kurt Galling, "Bethel und Gilgal," *ZDPV* 66 (1943): 144.

Ephraim during the chase (7:23-24). The report becomes credible if we understand Judg. 6:35 as an exaggerating addition. Then we would say that Gideon originally had behind him only the family of the Abiezrites, a Manassite clan (Josh. 17:2). The battle took place on the edge of the plain of Jezreel on the north slope of Gilboa.[17] If we have rightly reconstructed the details concerning the contingent, one admittedly would now hesitate to call the undertaking a holy war in the full sense of the word. At any rate, the collective activity of the tribes first begins only after the initial surprise victory by Gideon, thereby demonstrating that this is such a holy war; the joint effort also shows that a general amphictyonic interest was ascribed to the matter. This, however, precisely distinguishes the undertaking from that recorded in the second part of the narrative. Here it is a matter of blood vengeance, which is then also satisfied by the killing of the guilty "kings."

If the Gideon story shows us a clear tension between the historical details and the generalized conception of the literary portrayal, then the Jephthah story (Judg. 11) sets us completely within this problem.[18] Jephthah is originally the leader of a crowd of bandits, thus a professional soldier; and, as the story itself shows, in this capacity he was by no means unknown in his country. The way in which the elders of Gilead, in the distress brought upon them by the threat of Ammon, turned completely to him for help and how in the reciprocal negotiations he carefully stated the conditions for his response is clearly the exact opposite of the kind of spontaneous, spirit-driven appearance of those who became the leaders in holy wars. Likewise, the reference to the holy place of Mizpah and the statement that Jephthah "spoke" (i.e., "promised") all this "in the presence of [RSV 'before'] Yahweh" (Judg. 11:11) points primarily only to the sacral form of this agreement. Finally, it is striking that in the story itself, where one

17. Concerning the "Harod Spring" in Judg. 7:1, see Curt Weidenkaff, "Ist *'ên dschâlûd* die alttestamentliche Harodquelle?" *PJ* 17 (1921): 27-31.
18. Concerning the historical and territorial-historical background of the Jephthah story see Noth, "Das Land Gilead," 66ff.

would expect it, there is no report of a summoning of the tribes.[19]
And yet it would no doubt be wrong to set up too simple an
alternative ("either/or"). History really does create complicated
situations; and the way in which the Ephraimites of west Jordan
entered after the battle (Judg. 12:1) still seems thereby to indicate
that the incident had been understood—at least later—as an amphictyonic concern. Just as clear, however, is the fact that the
present portrayal of Jephthah as a charismatic has painted over the
historical reality in favor of a schema.

This criticism of the narrator's conception—especially the
fact that with only one exception in ch. 9 the book of Judges in
its present form speaks only of holy wars—leads us to the question
of whether on the whole all the wars of this time were actually
conducted as holy wars. That, however, could hardly be the case.
The history of the several tribes after the Conquest, the details of
which are now beginning to become clear to us through the territorial-historical works of Albrecht Alt and Martin Noth, was very
complicated. As a result of expansion or rounding out of territories,
or attacks from outside, or colonization, there took place an abun-
dance of local military embroilments of which no report has come
to us precisely because they were not holy wars. We should be all
the more thankful for the isolated account of Abimelech (Judg. 9).
Where, then, in the give-and-take of these battles was the amphictyony with its cult and their commitment to stand by one
another when summoned for holy war? This cultic activity was
certainly still existent, but the events which these majestic narrations report lay not at all, or at least not directly, within the specific,
cultic realm of influence. Thus, correspondingly, these non-cultic
military activities, carried out by mercenaries, were devoid of any
sacral consecration. The assumption that they might have been
carried out in the name of Baal-berit ("lord of the covenant") would
be absurd, even apart from the fact that Baals do not conduct holy

19. The reference to such a (futile) summoning in Judg. 12:2 is not entirely
convincing.

wars, and it finds not the slightest support in these very precise narratives.

Just as infrequently do we hear of any sacral calls-to-arms of the tribes in the many conquests of Canaanite urban enclaves which are to be presupposed on the basis of Judg. 1 alone. Such mopping up or such expansion activities seem to have belonged to the inner affairs of the separate tribes. These aggressive actions of the tribes are seldom accessible to us in firsthand accounts. That makes it all the more important to assess the report of the migration of the tribe of Dan and its conquest of Laish (Judg. 17–18), for here we see in an individual case such a battle of a tribe for its *Lebensraum,* conducted under the assistance neither of Israel nor of Yahweh.[20] The victory over Heshbon (Num. 21:21-31) can be ascribed to the tradition of a generalized Israel. Here we are dealing, however, with an individual activity of the tribe of Gad in the process of its expansion into the land east of Jordan,[21] and there is no reference to a levy of the amphictyony or a sacral form of carrying on the war.[22] Furthermore, the Old Testament itself gives us elsewhere a very instructive term for this kind of secular undertaking. Despite the fact that David and his people were involved only in a secular undertaking (דֶּרֶךְ חֹל), he and his people were

---

20. The questioning of Yahweh before the undertaking in Judg. 18:6 certainly does not speak against that.

21. Noth, "Israelitische Stämme zwischen Ammon und Moab," 38; *Aufsätze zur biblischen Landes- und Altertumskunde,* 1:414-15.

22. It has been demonstrated that the sequence of narratives in Josh. 1–9 shows only the conquest of the tribe of Benjamin (Alt, "Josua," 13-25; Kurt Möhlenbrink, "Die Landnahmesagen des Buches Josua," *ZAW* 56 [1938]: 239-240). This is now actually recounted in an accentuated way as a sacral undertaking. Although now also the Jericho saga (Josh. 6) and the Ai saga (Josh. 7) cannot be taken as immediate historical testimonies (Möhlenbrink, 258-262), very much of the sacral does still remain in this complex of traditions. That is obviously no surprise, since these are old sagas about holy places. But at the same time, the question whether the sacral components can be attributed simply to these traditions is not yet definitively answered. However, since the cultic tradition of the tribes in its pre-amphictyonic existence is still so consistently inaccessible to our knowledge, the question must remain open.

ritually pure and thus the priest could without hesitation give them holy bread to eat. The reference shows that in this respect very precise distinctions had been made in early times (1 Sam. 21:5).

*   *   *

With these observations we have already entered into general considerations of the historical phenomenon of holy war. Even for the time of the judges we are not able to let the sources speak to us uncritically, for, even though in this case the source relationships are incomparably more favorable than for the time of the Conquest or even earlier, still the tradition has unquestionably distorted the historical picture in that it holds holy wars to have been the ordinary and the normal. We again summarize what we have seen as the marks of such wars as actually carried on in a sacral form:

Obviously, the foremost characteristic of such a war is the emergence of the comprehensive sacral alliance. Despite the fact that in no single instance were the majority of the twelve tribes involved, these wars are still in principle portrayed as the response of the amphictyony, carried out in the name of Yahweh, who was not merely a tribal god but the God of "Israel." Second, these wars appear in fact to have been exclusively defensive wars.[23] In the case of the threat to the covenant of the tribes as a whole, the amphictyony's reaction is to be taken for granted. But even in cases in which only one tribe is menaced, the whole is appealed to for help without hesitation. This commitment of the whole to each individual member is expressed very beautifully in the assembly at Mizpah.

"One tribe is cut off from Israel this day. What shall we do for [them]?" (Judg. 21:6-7a)[24]

---

23. Caspari, 132. Here, therefore, the later portrayal of the Conquest in Josh. 1–9 errs particularly blatantly.

24. Covenant wars against a rebellious member of the amphictyony itself are also known from Greek history. Cf. Ulrich Kahrstedt, *Griechisches Staatsrecht* (Göttingen: Vandenhoeck & Ruprecht, 1922), 397.

Incidentally, the causes of the war were exactly as diverse as history could possibly provide. Among the acute political necessities which could lead to a holy war we must also consider the possibility that the origins [of a given tribe] might have played an important role in creating an obligation. With one people or tribe Israel may well have stood in an "oath of peace,"[25] while not with others. We do not know the reasons for this, and perhaps even the ancient Israelites did not always provide themselves with a rational explanation for this fact. The best-known case is Amalek: "Yahweh will have war with Amalek from generation to generation."[26] On the other hand, there is a certain tolerant reticence discernible in relation to Edom: it is spoken of as Israel's אָח ("brother").[27]

The army is recruited by the levying of the free farmers who would be called to arms by trumpet blasts and by messengers.[28]

25. [Editor's note: The term *Urfehde* is an oath to be at peace, an oath to renounce vengeance—in later times, an oath not to repeat a certain offense. At the same time, an *Urfehde* is a negative bondedness, as in "I have sworn never to be at rest until someone is avenged." Like the English word "feudal," it connotes the subject of commitment. It seems that von Rad uses *Urfehde* here without being aware of the great ambivalence between its positive and negative meanings.]

26. Exod. 17:16 [cf. Kurt Möhlenbrink, "Josua im Pentateuch: Die Josuaüberlieferungen ausserhalb des Josuabuchs," *ZAW* 59 (1942/43): 17]; Deut. 25:17; 1 Sam. 15:2.

27. Num. 20:14; Deut. 2:4, 8; Amos 1:11.

28. The amphictyonic army was composed of the separate tribal squads, and these were organized by "thousands" (אֲלָפִים) and by "hundreds" (מֵאוֹת) (2 Sam. 18:1, 4). A comparison between 1 Sam. 10:19 and 21 makes it appear that the "thousand" corresponds with the "family" (מִשְׁפָּחָה) (Josh. 7:16-17), as the word אֶלֶף has also elsewhere virtually the meaning of "family" (e.g., Judg. 6:15; 1 Sam. 23:23). If the large list of Num. 26:5-51 really stems from the time between Deborah and David and can be taken as an "index of the state at that time . . . an inventory of the old Israelite amphictyony" (Martin Noth, *Das System der zwölf Stämme Israels,* 130), then we have also a description of the way in which the amphictyonic army was built up, for the combat levy was nothing other than cultic in the more narrow sense. The fact that the list mentions also isolated communities in addition to the clan associations (e.g., Num. 26:31) is not surprising, for according to Amos 5:3 "cities" (i.e., local associations) could also join the army. The smallest unit was the "fifties" (חֲמִשִּׁים); cf. 2 Kgs. 1:9ff.; Isa. 3:3. An army that is "fiftied" (חֲמֻשִׁים) is completely organized, that is, ready for battle (Josh. 1:14; 4:12; Judg. 7:11).

Concerning the size of the armies we can hardly risk exact statements. The Song of Deborah speaks at one point, which has often
been taken seriously, of forty thousand warriors (Judg. 5:8), but
this can be really only understood as the maximum upper limit.
Saul should have first commanded six hundred and then three
thousand (1 Sam. 13:15; 14:2), and Gideon only three hundred in
his major battle (Judg. 7:16). To understand these figures, we must
remember that only in exceptional cases did the strategic potential
of the plains come into question as battle terrain.

Any Israelite could be recognized as leader of the militia if
only his rising up was validated by the Spirit of Yahweh.[29] In
principle this charisma would validate itself; but history shows
that just as often it was the actual deed that proved the charisma,
which then drew the other tribes along to a more belated participation. And herewith we come to the true sore point of the whole
institution of holy war. We have seen that the literary portrayal—
and surely not first that of the Deuteronomists, but already that of
the older narrators—does not view the military events as locally
limited incidents (which most of them were) but seeks to understand them as far as possible to be wars of all Israel, or at least of
a larger group of tribes. In the face of this attitude, we must be
surprised that despite the editorial tendency a welter of details
about the actual limited participation has still been preserved—

29. Unfortunately, the thoroughly Deuteronomistic revision of the tradition
no longer permits us to recognize the original designation for such a military
charismatic; there must have been such a title. This person certainly was not called
a "judge," because this title is nowhere at home in the old texts (Oskar Grether,
"Die Bezeichnung 'Richter' für die charismatischen Helden der vorstaatlichen
Zeit," ZAW 57 [1939]: 119), but belongs to the Deuteronomistic framework.
Rudolf Kittel (A History of the Hebrews, 2 [London: William & Norgate and New
York: G. P. Putnam's Sons, 1896]: 94 and 3-4) points to the קָצִין theme in Judg.
11:6, which clearly represented some kind of a military official in ancient times
(Josh. 10:24). But the text does not necessarily prove anything, since Jephthah,
as we have seen, was certainly no authentic charismatic. More likely is the מוֹשִׁיעַ,
which Grether has proposed (p. 120). But the proof passages for the participial
form (Judg. 3:9, 15), independent of the question of whether they are old, do not
really make it clear enough that this is the designation of an office.

facts in which the narrators, as said, were not at all interested. We find such indices most abundantly in the stories of the ark of the covenant (1 Sam. 4–6), in which almost all of the accompanying circumstances, historically so important for us, have been deprived of their specificity. These texts speak now only of "Israel" and not of what must have corresponded more with the historical reality of a contingent of a few particular tribes. Nor do they name the leader of this contingent. This is in keeping with the narrators' peculiar interest, which in this case is concentrated exclusively on the ark itself.[30]

Thus to the discerning historian the actual imperfection of this institution cannot remain hidden. The sacral bond was still too weak for the widely scattered tribes and their special interests. Moreover, the sporadically sparkling charisma of a person, until then completely unknown and without office, was a factor too inconstant to set in motion a truly viable and capable military

---

30. Leonard Rost, *The Succession to the Throne of David* (Sheffield: Almond, 1982), 6-34. In the time of the judges (i.e., the classical time of the holy wars), the ark would hardly have been carried along into the field. None of the war stories mentions it. If we set aside the accounts of Josh. 3ff. because from a historical point of view they are very suspect, then we first find the ark in wars in the later period (1 Sam. 4–6; 2 Sam. 11:11). But who can say what distant tribal traditions lie behind the sagas of the Benjaminite conquest. Here we will be all the more ready to let possibilities stand open. The "ark saying" (Num. 10:35-36) does bring the ark into connection with Yahweh's warlike behavior, but this text must certainly not be a formulation first from the time of Saul or David. So it will be hard to get clarity about the function of the ark in holy wars. The fact that at some time and somewhere such a connection once existed is, from Num. 10:35-36, beyond doubt. On the other hand, oddly enough, the accounts of the time of the judges lack any allusion to it; with this 1 Sam. 4:3 concurs, in that taking the ark along is acknowledged as an extreme measure. When we study cultic matters it is even more apparent than when we study historical facts; we are concerned with varied relationships and the diverse conceptions which lie behind them, which in the course of time have solidified themselves dogmatically. It is very questionable whether, as we always take it, we can ever trace a unity of the standing and relevant historical facts behind the present variety of the traditions. In any case, the narratives of Josh. 3–6 are not immediately based on historical fact, but rather on a definite tradition that already has become quite solidified, not only concerning the ark but also concerning the course of events of the Conquest itself.

organism and to hold it together. The tribes' "going it alone" which the book of Judges itself bewails—"each one did what pleased him" (Judg. 21:25)—was obviously more powerful than the feeling of belonging together.

Therefore, we deal here with a cultic institution which historically never became fully manifest in its essential and intended form.[31] But the negative side of these perhaps somewhat disappointing results of our historical reconnaissance does not in the end mean too much, for a sacral institution such as this does not truly have its existence only in its actual extrinsic consequences. The institution certainly did exist as such, for—however partial the undertakings may have been—each time it did contain ideally within itself the prototype of holy war. The faith-oriented subsoil, out of which these wars drew their strength, must have been a nearly inexhaustible supply, because the content which this institution left behind after its dissolution continued to fructify and to engage Israel yet many more centuries, as we shall see later.

Now, however, as we inquire into the ideological, religious foundation of the holy wars, we run into a nearly insoluble hermeneutical problem. The rites and practices were primeval. They existed both before and after our period, and they were also in use among other peoples. Comparative religion has explained the origins of this kind of ritual in primitive, magical thinking.[32] The result of this is that [modern] people have believed that the corresponding practices in ancient Israel must also trace their meaning back to their primitive magical understanding. That admittedly represents an unjustified extreme, just as the orthodox theocratic

31. This is probably why Max Weber recognizes only three wars as holy wars: Judg. 4–5; 20; 1 Sam. 11 (*Ancient Judaism* [Glencoe, Ill.: Free Press, 1952], 44). On the other side, Caspari goes much too far when he considers "every organized application of the force of arms" as a holy war (p. 142). [Editor's note: von Rad here dropped a significant word from Caspari's original statement: "As long as they are found in this situation, in fact every organized *joint* application of the force of arms appears to have been holy war and Yahweh's war."]

32. Friedrich Schwally, *Semitische Kriegsaltertümer,* 1: *Der heilige Krieg im alten Israel* (Leipzig: T. Weicher, 1901).

way of understanding them had been; for, when dealing with cultic practices, who would want to set their first, primeval meaning as the normative principle of interpretation for all later times? The Israel of the time of the judges, according to a very good formulation of Martin Buber, found itself spiritually in the condition of a "primitive pan-sacralism"—that is, it lived in a world of conceptions in which the whole space of the people's life was sacrally bound together.[33] All realms of life still rested equally in sacral orders, without the cult having occasion to set itself apart with a certain degree of autonomy, without "cult" and "life" being divided blatantly from one another. The concept of the primitive encompasses principally these two factors: a primary, collectively-determined way of thinking and acting, and a precritical, unreflective attitude toward the content of the cultic tradition. Thus our question, so concerned for interpretation of the sense of this or that rite of holy war, is no doubt misleading, for reflective interpretation of meaning was particularly foreign to that time. One did it this way and not otherwise, and was thereby sure of the presence and help of Yahweh.[34] Accordingly, in this difficult inquiry it is methodologically more advisable to begin with how in that time one imagined Yahweh and his way of ruling, rather than reconstructing the meaning from isolated practices, as comparative religion has done. Johannes Pedersen has portrayed the holy war as a great magical network of powers.[35] God is the source of the power; from God every individual warrior receives power. The task of the army

33. Martin Buber, *Moses: The Revelation and the Covenant* (Oxford: East and West Library, 1946), 120; repr. Atlantic Highlands, N.J.: Humanities, 1988.

34. This difficult problem can be clarified with reference to Exod. 17:11-12, the narrative of Moses' stretching out his arms to the battle. As the account is now narrated, we must think of some kind of a "victory of prayer" (Möhlenbrink, "Josua im Pentateuch," 19). But that will suggest to us only an already spiritualized interpretation of the event. However, how could we thoroughly apprehend the conception of the ancient faith in Yahweh? Comparative history of religions certainly can help, but it can as straightly lead us past the decisive element, of which Schwally's book is a warning example. [See above, n. 32.]

35. *Israel, Its Life and Culture,* 3:1-32.

leader is always the same: to increase this power, and this takes place only by connection to the source of power. Yahweh works in unity with the warriors, because he works with their souls. Holiness has its root in the soul; it is a universal power that fills all the men. Weapons are certainly important, but of much greater significance is the fact that those who used them possessed the proper power in the soul: "It is the powers, the invisible powers at work behind, which decide the issue."[36] But is that really true? The Song of Deborah knows nothing of this all-decisive stream of power and "psychic contest," and the spiritualizing Joshua narratives (Josh. 6), as drawn upon especially by Pedersen, know absolutely nothing either. No one will deny that there is an array of magical residues, but they are strikingly undercut by one factor which is far more dominant—namely, Yahweh's freedom and unpredictability, which no magical chain of power can bind. According to everything that we know, belief in Yahweh even in its archaic form had an eminently personalistic character, a component so strongly voluntaristic that even in its collectively-bound antiquity it held itself aloof from, if not bluntly antagonistic toward, that magical thinking. No, it is not powers which decide, but rather the צִדְקוֹת יהוה, Yahweh's "manifestations of salvation," as the Song of Deborah itself formulates it (Judg. 5:11). Moreover, in the fact that the stylized war narratives of a later time ascribe everything decisive to Yahweh and his intervention, they certainly concur with the ancient conception. This intervention, however, was personal, not effective through mediation of powers; rather, Yahweh himself was present, thundered, made stones to fall, the earth to shake, and so forth.

Trusting in this personal aid of Yahweh, Israel carried on its holy wars. It is as good as certain that the concept of faith—in other words, that confident trusting in the action of Yahweh—had its actual origin in the holy war and that from there it took its own peculiar dynamic character. Let us refer back again to the list on

36. Pedersen, 3:12-20.

page 45. Even if these sentences can all be regarded only indirectly as formulations of a later time, which was ripe for speaking as well of the object of the life of faith, yet this phrase "do not fear, but believe" is still with overwhelming unity the actual theme in all of the old war narratives. There is no reason to assume that because this theme became so endlessly varied that something originally foreign to it has been mixed into these traditions. Is it not characteristic that here, where a prophet updates this ancient sacral order for his time, immediately again there echoes the phrase "do not fear, but believe"?[37] One can put the question this way: Where else could this faith motif have had its *Sitz im Leben?* Originally it would certainly have been nowhere in individual life, but in something collective, which means in the cult. In the cult, however, it would not have fit in the context of the festal celebrations, but rather within the jurisdiction of the historical rule of Yahweh, which is what ancient Israel experienced only in its holy wars.

But we would be greatly misunderstanding these wars if we sought to comprehend them as religious wars in the sense that has become current for us—that is, as a conscious fighting for a religion. That they were not, at least not in the sense that they would have been carrying on a war against the gods of the enemies and their cults. It is very notable that in the Song of Deborah and in the other old traditions the gods of the enemies and their cultic sphere do not come into the field of vision at all. Indeed, we have seen that these wars lacked every offensive spirit. Neither the cult of the Amalekites or of the Ammonites and so forth, which would be irreconcilable with faith in Yahweh, served as the occasion or the object of the holy wars, but rather their attack against the outward political existence of Israel or one of its tribes. In other words, in the holy wars Israel did not arise to protect faith in Yahweh, but Yahweh came on the scene to defend Israel, for the members of the amphictyony were sheltered under his protection;

37. See Isa. 7:4 and below, 101ff.

Israel was Yahweh's possession.[38] We saw that the conquest by the tribes took place predominantly in peaceful ways. When the tribes, then, in the course of further historical developments suddenly experienced Yahweh's power also in the sacral form of wars, that was a new revelation of his essence. Thus, the beautiful observation of Wilhelm Caspari is confirmed, that the cry "Yahweh is a man of war" (Exod. 15:3) is to be understood in the sense of a discovery, a joyful surprise.[39]

After all the above, it is not easy to fix accurately the cultic ideological content of those old holy wars between the later theologizing portrayals, on the one hand, and an extreme primitive, magical understanding on the other. Yet the distinction is clear—namely, the cautious attitude with regard to the mythological; and that should make us think. There are no esoteric rituals which suggest a holy happening which takes place, so to speak, above the world of outward actions. What happens here—that is, what Yahweh does—happens right in the foreground and completely realistically. Even the rare statement about the stars sharing in the fight (Judg. 5:20), if not understood in general as poetic elaboration, does not refer to an actual mythological set of concepts. It lies, rather, along the line of those other natural activities (earthquakes, hailstones, thunder) which Yahweh occasionally caused.[40] Nowhere do we see what should theoretically have been a possibility—namely, a link with the myth of the combat with the dragon of chaos. Here we have finally succeeded in grasping something which was difficult for us to fix: one side of the really ancient faith in Yahweh even before its being interlaced with Canaanite mythological cultic traditions.

38. The Deuteronomic-Deuteronomistic conception of holy war is, on the other hand, different at this point. See below, 117-18.

39. Caspari, 128-29.

40. So it is certainly a misinterpretation when Pedersen understands the Kishon in the Song of Deborah not as an ordinary, but as a mythical river ("a primeval river") in *Israel*, 3:7.

CHAPTER 3

Holy War in the
Post-Solomonic Novella

TURNING NOW TO THE EARLY PERIOD of the kings, we find in the source literature which concerns our subject that, first of all, no noteworthy shift can be observed. Even Saul and David still carried on their wars to a great extent as holy wars. That need not at all be viewed suspiciously as a later literary, generalizing stylizing of the story. We remember that the holy wars were defensive wars and that the royal state specifically as an army kingship had come under political pressure from outside; so it is *a priori* to be assumed that the kingship as such, in its understanding of the *essence* of wars, still had brought no radical dismantling and reconstruction of the holy war. And yet, with the rise of kingship the end of the sacral institution of holy wars *in principle* was sealed, for the decisive shift which accompanied the rise of kingship in Israel was so deep and so momentous that it had to result in external and internal rearrangements in every realm of the people's life. We must first discuss several of the factors of this process of reformation, since only in this way is it possible to get a proper understanding of most of the narratives of the holy wars—particularly those of the time of Joshua and Judges—because surely these narratives first received their decisive formulation in the time of the Monarchy.

We begin with a reference to the outward changes in the nature of the army under Saul, David, and Solomon, and then will try to portray what is fundamental in the radically changed spiritual and

74

cultural atmosphere. It is self-evident that with this sequence we shall be saying nothing about the original dependence of inner things on outer ones. In this connection the sequence would certainly be the opposite. But in such far-reaching occurrences of restructuring in the life of a people there is no way to discern clearly what is cause and what is effect. If at any one time an epoch comes to its end, then the previous order is shaken from the depths in ways which do not yield to rational analysis. In any case, in this connection the question should be less raised about causes; the inquiry into the realities already offers us enough material and enough problems.

Saul's kingship was a definitive army kingship—little more than a constitutionally stabilized, charismatic leadership.[1] What was new, however, is that Saul began by creating a troop of professional soldiers. Obviously, the calling up of the old militia functioned clumsily and no longer sufficed for the higher strategic demands of the time. Saul needed troops permanently under arms.

> When Saul saw any strong man, or any valiant man, he attached him to himself. (1 Sam. 14:52)

The statement in 1 Sam. 13:2 that Saul "chose three thousand men of Israel" will likewise need to be understood in the sense that Saul kept a permanent bodyguard available. In itself, having mercenaries is not at all a new phenomena on Palestinian soil; it is as old as the culture of the city-states. Even in the stories of Abimelech and of Jephthah we also run into such professional soldiering (Judg. 11:3). The Philistines also waged their wars with mercenaries.[2] It was much rather the old Israelite way of waging war with a peasant militia that denoted something new. The contradiction between militia and professional soldiers is to a great extent a socio-economic opposition. The militia was formed of

1. Albrecht Alt, "The Formation of the Israelite State in Palestine," *Essays on Old Testament History and Religion* (Garden City: Doubleday, 1968), 223-309.
2. Alt, "Formation of the Israelite State," 235.

free farmers who could be expected to provide their own main-
tenance for the brief time of their military service;[3] the permanent
hireling had to be supported from public means (Judg. 9:4). Since
the tax structure of Saul's state presumably was yet at its very
beginning, most likely economic reasons would have been a major
hindrance to Saul in the development of a standing army.

The circumstances must have been different under David, for
quite suddenly the sources in this respect become very communica-
tive. David himself had arisen out of the institution of a military
retinue which Saul had founded. He had won a position of power
as leader of his troops first of all in the Judean south, and then
after he was chosen king over Israel he conquered Jerusalem "with
his mercenaries," as Albrecht Alt has taught us to understand it.[4]
And what we learn then of every "Tom, Dick, and Harry," of the
"thirty" (מִשְׁמַעַת) points to a military apparatus that is already
quite complex.[5] This militia/mercenaries dualism is also plainly
visible, for instance, in the account of the war against the Ammonites (2 Sam. 10:6–11:1; 12:26-31). This war is divided into
several strategic individual campaigns. First, the field captain Joab
moves out with the גִּבּוֹרִם, the professional soldiers.[6] After having
won the victory the unit turns back again to Jerusalem where it
was stationed. Later there is a completely different event: David
calls on the militia (וַיֶּאֱסֹף אֶת־כָּל־יִשְׂרָאֵל) and wages with it a
second victorious battle. The source is silent about the participation
of mercenaries. In a third phase, at "the time when kings go forth
to battle," David begins the final campaign against Ammon and
actually sends Joab out first. Joab commands, first, his own sol-

---

3. This is clearly described in 1 Sam. 17:17-18.

4. Alt, "Formation of the Israelite State," 283.

5. 2 Sam. 23:23 (Karl Elliger, "Die dreissig Helden Davids," *PJ* 31 [1935]:
66-75). David obviously led the wars against the Philistines with mercenaries
(2 Sam. 21:15ff.; 23:9ff.). Cf. Erhard Junge, *Der Wiederaufbau des Heerwesens
des Reiches Juda unter Josia. BWANT* 75 [4/23] (Stuttgart: Kohlhammer, 1937):
9.

6. The הַגִּבּוֹרִים in 2 Sam. 10:7b is perhaps an explanatory addition, but more
correct. The גִּבּוֹרִים are professional soldiers; cf. 2 Sam. 23:8-9.

diers and, secondly, "all of Israel," meaning the militia. The Bathsheba story (which is literarily independent of the report of the war against the Ammonites because it belongs to the larger literary unity dealing with the succession to the throne)[7] shows in Uriah's answer to David the same dualism:

> The ark and Israel and Judah are staying in tents, and my master Joab and my lord's men are camped in the open fields. . . . (2 Sam. 11:11 NIV)

This should be understood that, first of all, the mercenaries function as the bearers of the actual military event. But the militia has also been called up, only it stands yet at the phase of being billeted and apparently will stay ready for the decisive blow.[8] In any case, the stratification says much: the militia now is ranked behind the professional army in war! In the scene which David then plays out before the messengers, we also learn the special military designation for such a mercenary troop: they are the "king's servants" (עַבְדֵי הַמֶּלֶךְ), a guard personally subordinated to the king (2 Sam. 11:24). So one understands also that David is especially concerned not to have this experienced and costly troop unnecessarily endangered or diminished.

A further, more decisive building up of the professional army and thereby a further relegation of the militia to the background took place under Solomon; for now horses and chariots were introduced into the technology of war. The chariot combatants were, of course, especially trained professional soldiers. For these units, their horses, and chariots, specific cities had to be built up as fortresses. These were Hazor, Megiddo, [Gezer,] Beth-horon, Baalath, and Tamar, former Canaanite cities (1 Kgs. 9:17ff.). Ac-

---

7. Albrecht Alt, "Zelte und Hütten," *Alttestamentliche Studien Friedrich Nötscher,* ed. Friedrich Nötscher and Karl Th. Schäfer. Bonner biblischen Beiträge 1 (Bonn: Peter Hanstein, 1950): 22-23; repr. *Kleine Schriften,* 1 (Munich: C. H. Beck, 1959): 239-240.

8. For the literary analysis, cf. Leonhard Rost, *The Succession to the Throne of David,* 57-64.

cording to Erhard Junge, "What previously had been inimical to the entire Israelite way of being had now become the mainstay of the kingdom. Everything about it lay in the hands of the royal mercenaries."[9] Let us ask ourselves: could this band of soldiers—international or at least partly recruited out of previously Canaanite territories—understand their wars as a sacral event, as a mobilizing of the God of Israel? And if not, were there then two conceptions of war: among the mercenaries, a secular, and in the militia, a sacred? In fact, such a strange duality must have persisted for a while, for how could the militia, recruited out of patriarchally-ordered farmers, have ceased at one blow to understand war sacrally and have given up the ancient cultic rites? But in the time of David the problem was still hidden. We learn that the holy ark was with the militia and that Uriah—a professional soldier!—still took his ritual duties very seriously. Also, the beautiful word that Joab is supposed to have spoken in a very dangerous hour in the Ammonite war must be mentioned here:

> "Be strong and let us fight bravely for our people and the cities of our God. The LORD will do what is good in his sight." (2 Sam. 10:12 NIV)

Joab is the leader of the professional soldiers, but the war report shows him, in terms of faith, still bound to the old conceptions of holy war. On the other hand, it will also admittedly not be difficult to sense the remarkable distance between this sober, objective devoutness and the old sacral institution, even apart from the fact that the reference to the "cities of our God" would have been unthinkable in the amphictyonic time. However, how might this devoutness really have appeared in the garrison of the Canaanite-Israelite chariot cities?

In the very ancient story of the counting of the people (2 Sam. 24), we have a document which shows that people very soon became aware of this tension and that, at any rate, individual circles of the

---

9. *Der Wiederaufbau des Heerwesens,* 16.

people certainly took very critical measures in the reordering of the army. It is clear that the census of the people ordered by David had a military meaning. Obviously David wanted to have a "muster roll for recruitment," a written list of all those obligated for militia service. This, however, was a rationalizing and a mechanizing interference in the organism of holy war as a "miraculous improvisation,"[10] for an essential factor of the holy war was voluntariness— that is, the willingness worked by the Spirit of Yahweh. One can see from the account at what point the people's reaction began. It was not held against David that he set up a troop of professional soldiers. That did not directly touch either the militia or its sacral world. His contingent functioned, as we have seen, parallel to the militia and according to the old traditional style. But the conscription of those liable to militia service was an intervention—perhaps the first real one—in the old institution and left a deep impact in the people's memories.[11] The account of the rejection of Saul (1 Sam. 15) lets the contradiction break open very fundamentally. The account certainly preserves a correct recollection in saying that the king had actually come into conflict with the institutional forms of the holy war. However, the way in which it interprets this conflict as a battle between two absolutely mutually exclusive principles betrays clearly a later point of view, for the contradictions could not have broken into the open so fundamentally yet in the time of Saul. The narrative, which otherwise clearly appears to have originated at a later time, must therefore be dealt with in a different context.[12] A simple alternative, as we shall soon see, was first formulated by Isaiah, since in his time mobilization for and the waging of war had become an unambiguously secular matter.

---

10. Wilhelm Caspari, *Die Samuelbücher mit Sacherklärungen.* KAT 7 (Leipzig: A. Deichert, 1926): 663.

11. The fear of the censuses is widely represented. The comparison has often been proposed between 2 Sam. 24 and the *lustratio populi Romani* after the census by Servius Tullius (Livy i.44). For additional history of religions material, see Rosa R. Schärf, *Die Gestalt des Satans im Alten Testament* (diss., Zurich, 1948), 163ff.

12. See below, 94ff.

The old sacral form of waging war was, therefore, abandoned by means of a progressive internal erosion already through the transformation of the military institution at the beginning of the Monarchy until—strangely enough again at the point of a reorganization of the military institution under Josiah—it experienced a surprising renaissance.[13] Already these observations concerning technical changes in military organization help us grasp an important presupposition for the understanding of all of the narrations of holy wars from the book of Joshua up to the books of Samuel. Undoubtedly, much old material is contained in these accounts, and yet it may be regarded as proven that none of these narrators is himself to be dated before the early Monarchy. Nevertheless, it can be said that no one—and that means neither the narrators nor their listeners—was yet acquainted out of his own experience with real holy wars as Israel at the time of the judges waged them. And that will be fully confirmed for us later. This knowledge of the internal and external distance of the narrators from their subjects now challenges us with a very pressing question: what exactly lay between the events and the telling about them and gave those narrators a changed perspective?

Certainly more intervened than that change in the pattern of military organization. There occurred in between the events and the telling the enormous expansion of the old territory of the tribes to the powerful kingdom of David, whereby large Canaanite areas had been incorporated into the kingdom of Israel. Administratively, Solomon organized Israel internally into twelve territories for the purpose of taxation; thus, the governmental apparatus and the presence of the kingship became very keenly perceptible everywhere, even out in the countryside. Solomon had built his majestic edifices, and the temple had become a cultic center of Israel through the installation of the ark of the covenant. In addition, under Solomon Israel had begun to establish far-reaching commercial connections; with these a more refined life-style was introduced into the land. Israel began

13. See below, 124ff.

to participate as an equal member within the ranks of the Near
Eastern states, and diplomacy began to spin its webs. What a change
over against the times of Deborah and Gideon! And still the most
decisive factor is not yet named.

The era of Solomon was the time of a typical enlightenment.
In nearly all areas of life, it shows us an emancipation from the
old patriarchal commitments. The time of the "primitive pan-
sacralism" was definitively at an end. The change would be hardly
conceivable, had it not been that into the heart of the Israel at that
time, into the amphictyonic cult, a crisis had entered, a kind of
exhaustion and aging. The picture of the spiritual stagnation and
unbridled wickedness in Shiloh that is drawn for us in 1 Sam. 2
and 3 says enough. Perhaps even more explicit is the silence of
the sources concerning the destruction of Shiloh. The ancient place
of holy pilgrimage disappeared, apparently leaving no grave void!
This was also the time in which the old, formerly reverently-
believed ἱεροὶ λόγοι ("sacred words") were freed from the holy
places and attained literary form, which could be fitted in like
building bricks into large narrative compositions.

A chapter in its own right is the influx of international wisdom.
Undoubtedly wisdom first appeared in ancient Israel as a still
essentially non-theological, class-related ideal for shaping
character—that is, as a way of instructing young people of the
capital city's official class in good behavior, in right speech and
right silence, and concerning the right ways of dealing with friends,
with women, and with money. However, wisdom also encom-
passed aspects of natural history. When the annalist reports that
Solomon spoke about trees, great animals, fish, birds, and worms,
that means, of course, that we should be thinking especially of the
Gattung of the numbers proverbs, the great age of which is un-
questionable.[14] They represent the first effort to categorize according to conceptual groups natural peculiarities and mysteries. The

---

14. Prov. 30:15ff. (Albrecht Alt, "Die Weisheit Salomos," *ThLZ* 76 [1951]:
139-143; repr. *Kleine Schriften*, 2 [Munich: C. H. Beck, 1953]: 90-99).

proverbs are therefore the expression of a completely unmytho-
logical, much more objective desire to understand nature. The
speaker in such proverbs is a human being who has become confident of his comprehension, who rationally takes charge of his
environment and seeks to order it conceptually. All in all, this older
wisdom is rightly to be described as a pronouncedly formative
ideal which serves the cultivation of the individual. Of course,
such an educational ideal will first have been fostered in the court
and among the upper class of the capital city, but these various
considerations lead indeed to the assumption that wisdom was
democratized relatively early.

The most frequent and most pressing admonition in the older
Wisdom Literature has to do with the cultivation of the word.[15] In
important moments of life, to be able to speak appropriately and
impressively probably counted as the principal sign of an educated
person. Particularly in this art of speech, many of our narrators
allow their *dramatis personnae* to perform brilliantly. It is known
how the author of the Succession narrative skillfully dramatizes
the course of events by inserting speeches; and that is precisely
the technique of many of the narratives of the holy wars as well.
Some kind of close connection must exist between the instructions
in the proper rhetoric of wisdom and the artistic rhetoric of these
narrators, who certainly were not all from Jerusalem. This rhetoric
had a high cultural value, which was cultivated in broad strata of
Israel. Neither form-critically nor according to its theme (i.e., the
doctrine of the commonplaces) has this literature been adequately
made the object of our research.[16]

To this we add the description with which the young David
is recommended to King Saul as page, a portrayal which is admittedly an anachronism for the time of Saul:

15. Examples from the older Wisdom Literature include Prov. 23:9; 25:9,
11, 15; 26:4-5; 27:11; 29:20.

16. Martin Buber cites two examples (2 Sam. 14:13ff.; 20:16ff.) showing
most impressively the high level of shaping in such speeches (*Kampf um Israel*
[Berlin: Schocken, 1933], 107ff.).

"Behold, I have seen a son of Jesse the Bethlehemite, who is skilful in playing (יֹדֵעַ נַגֵּן), a man of valor (גִּבּוֹר חַיִל), a man of war (אִישׁ מִלְחָמָה), prudent in speech (נְבוֹן דָּבָר), and a man of good presence (אִישׁ תֹּאַר); and the LORD is with him (יהוה עִמּוֹ)." (1 Sam. 16:18)

Here we have the nobility of character (καλοκἀγαθία) of a young Israelite man of high position. The assumption therein is that he belongs to the class of free landowners. Beside the skill in musical art stands the training for war. A fine outward appearance must recommend him, but above all he must have mastery of the art of speech. The last and most important, admittedly, no one can acquire on his own; it is either there or not there: the blessing of Yahweh. He who is so identified is someone who as a young man grew up out in the Judean countryside! We grant that the narrator here is reporting a special case and that he commensurately intensifies the idealized qualities, but that does not mean that he arbitrarily applies a standard for comparison by which they could not be fundamentally measured.

What concerns us here is a sufficient cultural-historical awareness and a conceptual ordering of the era of Solomon. The distinctive marks of the new spiritual life, which we can only summarily note, were these: enlightenment, adoption of an educational ideal, cultivation of the individual, attention to rhetoric, new interest in the natural sciences. The spiritual epoch thereby inaugurated can still be communicated best by the phrase *Solomonic humanism*. The outward conditions, on which such a refined form of spiritual life tends to be dependent—peace, prosperity, a certain international exchange—were present. Indeed, it would have been surprising if things had gone otherwise in Israel. "Humanism," as used here, however, includes above all a strong literary assiduousness; without this factor it would be senseless to speak of a humanism. At work in this literary productivity now is a strange intertwining of creativity and dependence. Also, the Solomonic humanism stands on the tradition of an old venerable epoch, the content of which and the formation of which it has renovated

creatively—perhaps without full consciousness of its own different quality. This historical reaching back to an "antiquity" is virtually constitutive for the concept of humanism. Characteristic of
this productivity, above all, is its severing itself from the old sacral
connections to describe what is human.

This is, therefore, the phenomenon which stood between the
old holy wars and the people who told about them! We could
not describe the narratives of the book of Judges and 1 Samuel
as "sagas"; rather, they should really be regarded as novelistic—
that is, as a very cultivated artistic prose which undoubtedly uses
much ancient traditional material, but is as well just as free to
lift up the spiritual meaning of the events and at the same time
to transpose them into personal and human categories. A symp-
tom, if only occasionally discernible yet especially characteristic
for this completed spiritual transformation, is a tendency toward
sensitivity. The narrators know how to touch the reader. The
conclusion of the narrative of the rejection of Saul (1 Sam.
15:34b) and especially the touching narrative about David and
Jonathan (1 Sam. 20) are directed to a sensitive readership.
However, this narrative style so obviously derived from Solomonic humanism has sovereign freedom in the selection and
mastery of the most diverse stylistic devices. The scale ranges
from the high severe style of human tragedy (1 Sam. 15) to
burlesque (the Nabal story, 1 Sam. 25; and some of the Samson
narratives). It seems important to us to have determined the
spiritual location of the ancient narrators in this way in the face
of the process, gaining ground today, to primitivize and mytholo-
gize these materials. Thus, a whole world lies between those
wild warriors with their archaic rituals and conceptions from the
early time of Israel and the cultivated and expressly spiritual
atmosphere of these narrators who have never really experienced
holy wars.[17] In detail we lack now only a few more characteristic

---

17. "The ground which these reports offer looks more solid than it is. Probably
the Elohist was already only a layman" (Wilhelm Caspari, "Was stand . . . ?" 123).

clues; an analysis of all of the narratives called into question
would lead us much too far.

a. The account of the capture of Jericho (Josh. 6) in its present
form has been heavily cluttered literarily. Readers have always
found it especially troublesome that one account reports the
people's processing around the city quietly six times and then a
war shout on the seventh day, but another speaks of a trumpet blast
with each round. In addition, from a form-critical point of view,
two etiologies contradict one another in the narratives: the Rahab
etiology (v. 25) and the curse which brings about the devastation
of Jericho (v. 26). Should the discrepancies be explained by assuming a weaving together of two parallel sets of stories[18] or by
assuming that additions were gradually attached to a single account?[19] We need not be overly concerned with determining which
of these possibilities is more likely, for neither Martin Noth nor
Otto Eissfeldt have considered them to be additions that would
have distorted the text.

Those who fight against Jericho in the narrative are without
exception and unambiguously called the בְּנֵי יִשְׂרָאֵל. In no place
in this respect is there the trace of any discrepancy, although in
so many of the narratives of the judges, as in palimpsest, the more
restricted outline of what actually happened is discernible behind
the generalized conception. The narrator is of the conviction that
"Israel" *en masse* crossed the Jordan and then attacked Jericho.
However, that makes it clear that the relationship of this narrative
to the actual events of history was in any case quite disconnected.
The distant news which underlies his report no doubt has taken
a long path and has multifariously changed until it received its
present form from our present narrator. Characteristic for this
form is the strong and undoubtedly unhistorical stylization of the
event and the accentuation of the purely miraculous. This miracle

18. Otto Eissfeldt, *Hexateuch-Synopse* (1922; repr. Darmstadt: Wissen-
schaftliche Buchgesellschaft, 1962), and otherwise Kurt Möhlenbrink, "Die Landnahmesagen des Buches Josua," 258-59.

19. Martin Noth, *Das Buch Josua,* 34-43.

is absolute; over against it, no human activity belongs at all. That the narrative is founded on very ancient conceptions of magical enchanting influence is a correct assumption. However, it is also certain that the narrator no longer thinks of such magical activity. It should rather be said that this magical conception stands directly counter to the narrator's own because it presupposes once again a very concentrated activity on the side of the besieging force. For our author, however, Yahweh's action in the miracle is absolutely autarkic. Obviously, the narrator experiences the pressure of a strongly theoretical—theological—basic idea; he wants to give vivid expression to that concept.[20] On the other hand, however, the narrative is pronouncedly authentic in its rigorous objectivity regarding the ancient event. Nowhere is the subjective attitude of the fighters brought into the field of vision in any psychologizing way as actually happens in many of these stylized narratives. Also, the significance which is ascribed to the ḥērem command is antique, for of all the elements of the old holy wars this is the one that died out the soonest in the later novelistic writing.

b. An essentially different type of war story is represented by the account of Gideon's victory over the Midianites (Judg. 7). This account as well is literarily uneven. Whether the reference to the torches and jars in addition to the trumpets can justify the assumption that there are two different strands of narration is dubious. The only real parallels which stand over against each other are verses 21 and 22. For that reason alone the account should be evaluated differently from the preceding one, since it has no etiological intentions whatsoever; it is a historical novella and as such is less purposeful than an etiologically-oriented account. Furthermore, the historical event lies centuries nearer to the narrator than in the case of the Jericho story. But precisely for that

20. The account of Josh. 6 "appears [incidentally] as such a clear and deliberate narrative that hardly anything needs to be proved with regard to the technique of the old bards" (Caspari, "Was stand . . . ?" 121).

reason we are impressed by the uniformity of the conceptualization of the event, which can only be explained as coming from a general, basic theological perspective common to these narrators and their time. Also, the assumption of any kind of human synergism is carefully dismissed here. The warriors persist in their encirclement of the camp, and with their odd gestures they go to the point of the absurd. Yet within that sphere in which no Israelite sets foot, Yahweh alone is active with his miracles. This is obviously a very strongly theologically stylized conception. The ancient warriors in the time of the judges certainly did not believe any less in Yahweh's help in the holy war and in his miracles, yet nevertheless they fought hard. They came "to help" Yahweh, as the Song of Deborah suggests with great theological simplicity (Judg. 5:23). Thus, we first encounter here in the work of these post-Solomonic novella writers that understanding by which holy war and the absolute miracle of Yahweh are inseparably bound— indeed, are one and the same thing.

In contrast to the Jericho story, however, we encounter a new element in the prehistory of the actual miracle. It is true that Josh. 6 also recognizes a delaying, tension-heightening preparation for the miracle, but here the prehistory is concerned with the subjective attitude of the warriors. The reflection about self praise already betrays the narrator's location in a somewhat problematic situation of transition; for him and his listeners, accordingly, there is yet the possibility of a completely different secular understanding of the events, a possibility which certainly did not exist for Gideon's warriors. A further shift of interest toward the subjective-human attitude is brought by the passage concerning the elimination of the fearful and the account of the dream of the Midianites which should personally strengthen Gideon and give him certainty in the face of the great paradox. Thus, here the human perspective, with its hesitating or trusting attitude toward the action of Yahweh, has entered the narrator's field of vision and, in addition to the objective miracle, has become problematic in its own right. However, what most clearly separates our account from the real holy wars is most difficult to formulate precisely: it is the strongly secular and non-cultic spirit that penetrates the whole. If we think we can grasp something of the essence of the old sacral wars, it is precisely that this cool, almost enlightened "Protestant" atmosphere is quite foreign to its original pan-sacralism. That our narrator shows no interest at all in the cultic consecration of the booty is certainly no accident.

c. The narrative of the miracle of the sea (Exod. 14) is unquestionably woven together from parallel recensions. The elements which interest us here run more or less parallel in J and E. The account is actually not etiological; but, with regard to the great distance of the narrator from the event itself and the conclusions which follow from that, what was said about Josh. 6 applies. Here as well, the miracle is absolutely autarkic. There already is, in fact, a whole network of miracles that are offered for Israel's salvation. According to the Yahwist, instead of leading, the column of clouds moves protectively at the end of the host; an east wind drives the sea back. Yahweh looks on the Egyptian army and brings it into confusion. The wheels of the chariots become mysteriously mired, and ultimately the sea swallows up the enemies. For the technique of the portrayal, the piling up of speeches is especially characteristic. We are told what the Egyptians say to each other (Exod. 14:3, 5b, 25b), the apprehensive doubts of the Israelites (vv. 11-12), Moses' consoling response (vv. 13-14), and finally Yahweh's words to Moses (v. 26). It is self-evident that these discourses powerfully shift the event over onto a spiritual level. However, that does not occur at the expense of the real drama; it is rather something added, as is the case when we are dealing with narrators who are capable of going back and forth as they wish between the drama of the outward events and the processes of the psychological. What is so new and daring as far as this psychic drama is concerned is that the narrator portrays Israel as fearful, indeed as desperate and almost blaspheming (whereas the Gideon account had separated out the fearful as unsuitable warriors!). This inner inadequacy of Israel is obviously a very effective instrument of contrast. Above all, however, it gives the occasion to express in advance, through the mouth of Moses, the meaning of the immediately imminent miraculous event:

> "Fear not, stand firm, and see the salvation of the LORD, which he will work for you today; for the Egyptians whom you see today, you shall never see again. The LORD will fight for you, and you have only to be still." (Exod. 14:13b-14 [J])

This speech is programmatic in every respect: Israel participates in the event only as spectator. They should "stand there" and be still—that is, fearless and submissive to take note of the miracle. Precisely that is what these accounts are about: taking note. It is, after all, one of the main intentions of the text to make the reader also aware of the full significance of the miraculous event. A strong theological reflection stands as the driving force behind these accounts. The closing sentences offer a beautiful example of the well-balanced concern for both the objective and the subjective—that is, interest in the fact that ultimately Israel also subjectively understood the event with clear consciousness as a miracle of Yahweh and accepted it as such.

> Thus the LORD saved Israel that day from the hand of the Egyptians. . . . And Israel saw the great work which the LORD did against the Egyptians, and the people feared the LORD; and they believed in the LORD and in his servant Moses. (Exod. 14:30-31 [J])

How the situation has changed! In the old holy war only believers could take part. By virtue of their faith they carried the event from the beginning to the end. Here it is Yahweh who works the miracle, and Israel believes afterward. What is new, in short, is that the narrator also extends his interest to include the human experience of the enemies. Moreover, their inner attitude, the motives for their action, and the effect of the event on them have become issues to the narrator. It is really unusual that he places the decisive confession in the mouth of the perishing enemy and not Israel:

"Let us flee from before Israel; for the LORD fights for them against the Egyptians." (Exod. 14:25b [J])

d. The account of David's battle with Goliath (1 Sam. 17) is unquestionably the glittering jewel in this group of spiritualized war narratives. In it we find all of the previously-noted characteristics elevated to the highest art form. It can be considered as proven that as the text now lies before us it is composed of two versions which do not quite agree with one another (version A is 17:12-30 and 17:55–18:5; version B is 17:1-11, [31,] 32-54). As to age we cannot distinguish the two versions from one another. Version A is quite secular, and the religious points are clustered in B; but we must not draw major conclusions from this because the high point of the battle has not been preserved for us in version A. Common to both versions is the transposition of almost the entire event into the spiritual level of the speeches. The combined narrative contains eighteen shorter or longer direct speeches! Masterful are the manner in which the portrayal delays again and again before the battle, the concentration on the inconspicuousness of David, and, above all, how in the statement of the older brother the coming event is given an interpretation which borders on unbelief: it is David's arrogance (זָדוֹן, 17:28; RSV "presumption"). Finally, the first reference to Yahweh comes from David's mouth in the conversation with Saul (v. 37a). Saul does pick up the thought (v. 37b), but the interlude concerning armor shows that he also has failed to understand David. Immediately before the great turn in the battle, our narrator delivers the programmatic interpretive word, which certainly has already been framed here almost as a sermon:

"You come to me with a sword and with a spear and with a javelin; but I come to you in the name of the LORD of hosts, the God of the armies of Israel, whom you have defied.[21] This day

---

21. "In the name of" scarcely means "mandated by," but rather "as the property of," "under the sovereignty of."

the LORD will deliver you into my hand, and I will strike you down, and cut off your head; and I will give the dead bodies of the host of the Philistines this day to the birds of the air and to the wild beasts of the earth; that all the earth may know that there is a God in Israel, and that all this assembly may know that the LORD saves not with sword and spear; for the battle is the LORD's and he will give you into our hand." (1 Sam. 17:45-47)[22]

Here we find condensed once again almost the entire ideology of holy war. But how deeply everything has been changed! Now holy war and the use of weapons are antitheses, which generally exclude one another—a conception which the troops under Barak and Deborah would certainly not have understood. That Goliath is not at all immediately destroyed by a miracle of Yahweh, that it actually requires a sling, is certainly an inconsistency for which the narrator has to give his explanation. It is, in fact, surprising now that after the programmatic speeches the narrator reports no miracle, at least not one according to the traditional interpretation. What according to the older conception was an impenetrable divine mystery, which could scarcely be described, is now detailed realistically and soberly in broad daylight (vv. 48-50). This demythologization shows, however, how things have shifted for our narrator: for the narrator, the miraculous event itself is not even the high point of the story. The decisive "event" is far more the confessing word of David. And this word is spoken to Israel so that Israel might believe. Indeed, the help of Yahweh now finally aims directly at Israel's faith (v. 47). Previously God's aid was given exclusively to free Israel from some sort of political distress. The strong didactic intensifying of the whole thing here is evident. Thus, the correct attitude and conception of holy war are now focused paradigmatically in an individual, and this individual person gives a lesson to unbelieving and fearful Israel. In these and other characteristics to which our narrator turns, the spirit of the

22. We may ask whether v. 46b is not a parallel to v. 47a. Also, the double beginning of Goliath's speech in vv. 43 and 44 is text-critically dubious.

times is reflected clearly enough.[23] Not only have holy wars now become very foreign to this time, but also the relation of our narrator to the old reality has become more a literary and strongly spiritualizing one.

*   *   *

The four accounts just sketched can serve as types of a far greater number which, despite many dissimilarities in detail, still form a large family. We do not know the locations or the bearers of this high narrative culture; we can only say with certainty that they are characterized by the Solomonic and post-Solomonic humanism. The sequence of the types from *a* to *d* [as presented above] is not to be understood in all circumstances in the sense of a historical "evolution"; rather, it should simply indicate the existing broad spectrum in the extent of the spiritualizing. Common to all of the accounts is the strong thrust to lift the events out of the realm of the sacral and cultic. When we remember that the old holy war was a cultic organism of rites and practices, then we can see in these accounts no actual descriptions of holy wars at all. They deal much more with a novelistic-spiritualizing arranging of individual motifs which had been preserved in the tradition.[24] Precisely the failure to understand the archaic cultic character [in the early wars] led in these [later] accounts to such a reduction to the most decisive moment of the saving deed of Yahweh. We further saw how in

23. We can, for instance, recognize a shift in the direction of the more human in the fact that in his great address David speaks of the mocking of Israel (and not of Yahweh). Also, the conclusion is significant: the account does not end according to the old pattern with the objective fact of the victory, but with the founding of the friendship with Jonathan.

24. The use of these motifs, however, was not in any way restricted at the time and in the hand of our narrator to the accounts of real wars. They were already removed to such an extent from their original *Sitz im Leben* that they could also penetrate into completely different traditional materials. An example of how such a motif could become virtually decisive for the complete reworking of an old tradition is offered by the narrative of the spies, which varies widely to project the theme of despondency/faith. Cf. Num. 14:8-9, 11 (לֹא־יַאֲמִינוּ).

this narrative literature the equating of holy war with the absolute Yahweh miracle, which excludes any human collaboration, has been successfully imposed. This concept is therefore not "old"; it will preoccupy us again when we get to Isaiah. Over against this miracle, however, the narrator no longer presupposes a naive believing acceptance; we rather sense behind the narrative a strong theological reflection and the effort to make doubting and fearing human beings conscious of the miracle. In so far as the accounts are so pointedly aimed at faith and its strengthening, we have to consider relatively slight their real historic interest in the revivifying of a great past. All the more weighty is their actual didactic and kerygmatic concern.

CHAPTER 4

Holy War in the Prophets

WE BUILD UPON THE FOREGOING by first dealing with one of the spiritualized accounts of holy wars, one which certainly has a particular explanation, for the sake of which it must be somewhat disassociated from the other accounts: the narrative of Saul's battle with the Amalekites and his rejection (1 Sam. 15). The question of the status of this chapter in the great literary composition of the first book of Samuel does not interest us here; it suffices to observe that this also was originally an independent text. Literarily it is not a unified whole; certainly vv. 25-30a must be evaluated as a secondary expression which moderates the word about Yahweh's repentance (v. 29).[1] Since here primarily the narrator's conception of the events interests us much more than the historic events themselves, the question of the historicity of the events recounted can remain on the margin.

In that connection various misgivings surface: holy wars were defensive wars; they arose always in concrete situations of need and not so much out of historical-theological reflections, as suggested in v. 2. What Saul was searching for strategically in the deep south is a question in its own right, which admittedly need not automatically be answered negatively; but the few place

---

1. So Artur Weiser, "I Samuel 15," *ZAW* 54 (1936): 4. Others separate vv. 17-21, 24-26, 29 [Alfred Jepsen, *Nabi: Soziologische Studien zur alttestamentlichen Literatur und Religionsgeschichte* (Munich: C. H. Beck, 1934), 105 n. 1]. Again different is Richard Press, "Der Prophet Samuel: Eine traditionsgeschichtliche Untersuchung," *ZAW* 56 (1938): 206.

names are not at all able to diminish the colorlessness of the account.[2] The narrator obviously does not know anymore much that is concrete about the Amalekites, and least of all does he know about the kind of thing which would normally tend to be most firmly held in memory—namely, information about the battle itself.

The proportions in the narrative are especially striking. It recounts a war and its aftermath. The war is reported in the first nine verses, and the aftermath in the following thirty-six verses! Obviously the report of the war is only a kind of exposition; the narrator needs it only as a construct and inner motivation for the conflict story. As far as the style of the portrayal itself is concerned, it comes from the pen of one who, as we have seen already in other texts, is able to couch the entire drama in dialogue and who enables the reader also to experience after him the depths of the human tragedy without losing sight of the theological dimension. The conflict situation itself, however—whatever Samuel may have been historically—is portrayed as a paradigmatic conflict between king and prophet, and as truly originating in one of the demands of holy war. Indeed, when compared to similar accounts, our chapter already distinguishes itself formally through a series of prophetic style forms which give it a quite specific character, and for that reason this text must be taken by itself.[3] In the face of the *logion* in vv. 22-23 we must ask whether we should not classify under the *Gattung* of the prophet story the narrative which elaborately surrounds it like an artistic frame. The *logion* itself is stylized according to the type of the "debate speech," and it seems to take up a problem which has arisen. That would then clinch what on other grounds already appeared likely—namely, that the *logion* had had a life of its own before the framing of our narrative, and that it was then fused into the context of the narrative in such

2. In this kind of literature a borrowing of the place names from Gen. 25:18 would not be unthinkable.

3. v. 10. וַיְהִי דְבַר יהוה אֶל; v. 1; כֹּה אָמַר יהוה, v. 2; אֹתִי שְׁתָּלַח יהוה.

a way as to give it a broader meaning.[4] Thus, we may not interpret exactly stroke by stroke and word for word what is said about what Saul did and did not do, for only in a very broad sense does the proverb belong in the context of the narrative. A certain tension between the proverb and the narrative is especially perceptible in the fact that the point at which Saul was disobedient, the devotion (ḥērem) of the booty, was indeed a cultic requirement.[5] Admittedly, our narrator no longer regards it as such, for he indeed does not at all have a right understanding of the sacral organism of holy war anymore. Of the entire complex of rituals, only the ḥērem command is important to him; he absolutizes that command, and only around it and its being disregarded by Saul does he build the entirety of his story. That belongs together with the *Tendenz* of the narrative, which so strongly broadens the events into the paradigmatic. The actual historical interest of the narrator is obviously very slight, and we must ask whether the story in its details yields anything substantial about the historic understanding of Saul. Even the question of the motives of his action remains somewhat open. Likewise the way in which Samuel is conceived of as a *nabi* does not commend the account as a genuine source for reconstructing either the relationship of Saul to the historical Samuel or the political and historical situation of that time.[6]

But in its main concern the account, although also strongly generalized, does after all preserve one memory of overarching clarity: immediately after its emergence the kingship came into an insoluble conflict with the patriarchal standards of faith in Yahweh. And according to what we know about the development of the military order, it is only consistent that this conflict between the old faith in Yahweh and the kingship broke out first in the sphere of the

---

4. Weiser (10-11) thinks otherwise that v. 23b is prose and forms a bridge between the proverb and the account.

5. Carl H. Cornill, "I Sam. 15:22," *ZAW* 35 (1915): 62.

6. So perhaps Rudolf Kittel, *Gestalten und Gedanken in Israel: Geschichte eines Volkes in Charakterbildern*, 2nd ed. (Leipzig: Quelle & Meyer, 1932), 110-18. However, also Weiser, 18-21; and Press, "Der Prophet Samuel," 218-225.

prescriptions for holy war. Thus, after all, 1 Sam. 15 is also a document of that crisis which pervaded the end of the time of the judges
and the beginning of the time of the kings. The narrator names Saul
(and occasionally, standing behind Saul, "the people") the adversary
of the prophet; he means what we call "the state," that new political
entity in which Israel had pupated itself, still capable of development
and full of future potential, but already in its beginnings no longer
willing to let its behavior be prescribed uniquely by the laws of
Yahweh. Yet in this battle between two principles of whose definitive
sharpness our account is fully conscious, it is Yahweh who conquers;
his governance of history rolls on over that of Saul. Yahweh already
knows about the anointed one, "who is better" (v. 28). It can hardly
be the case, however, that in the time of Saul this conflict was
experienced so absolutely paradigmatically and so theologically as it
is here portrayed. Our account presupposes a very broad experience
and a condensed reflection about this problem. The spiritual locus of
such reflection and such polemic was, however, the prophetic movement, out of which our narrative undoubtedly stems. Thus we have
here a first proof that the prophetic movement understood itself as
custodian of the patriarchal order of the holy war. This knowledge
can, however, be significantly broadened.

*   *   *

What may have been spoken when the disciples of the prophets
"sat before Elisha" (2 Kgs. 4:38; 6:1)? We do not know what
Yahweh tradition was cultivated by them because their prophetic
function is so seldom reported in words of prophetic utterance.
Was it already the specifically eschatological concepts which we
encounter in the [later] writing prophets—of the day of Yahweh,
of cosmic and universal historical catastrophes? What the books
of Kings tell us about the messages of these prophets does not
seem to indicate that.[7] But what kind of picture would we have of

---

7. Apart from the complex of the Elijah and Elisha stories, one can get a little
material from the prophet narratives in 1 Kgs. 13, 20, 22 and 2 Kgs. 1, 3, 9–11.

the message of Isaiah if all we had available were the legends of
Isa. 36–39? Furthermore, we have to remember that the נְבִיאִים of
the ninth century can hardly be thought of as an essentially unified
movement. Yet a vital interest in what we call politics and from
time to time a crucial intervention belonged to the essential characteristics of north Israelite prophecy in this early time. Thereby it
viewed the historical events and the movements of the people of
God exclusively from the point of view of the will of Yahweh, his
good pleasure or displeasure. Prophecy itself, however, felt that it
was called in the name of Yahweh to provide the decisive impe-
tuses to action from case to case or to prevent what was displeasing
to Yahweh. Since, however, in those times the political and the
military activities were not yet separated, we will not be surprised
to encounter these prophets in the midst of military events as well
(cf. 2 Kgs. 3). On the other hand, it cannot be taken for granted,
for the old movement of ecstatic prophets shows no connection
whatsoever with the holy wars. In fact, when the charismatic
figures were leading their wars, there were as yet no נְבִיאִים in
Israel at all. Thus, it must be the case that in the ninth century we
are observing a secondary appropriation of old Yahweh traditions.
Now the prophets become the bearers and the proclaimers of
traditions that have already almost died out among the people. It
is well known, for instance, how they provided the impetus to the
campaign of Ahab against Ramoth in Gilead (1 Kgs. 22:11-12,
16). Thus, that is truly still a proclamation of the holy war (קִדְּשׁוּ
מִלְחָמָה, Mic. 3:5b). However, with that the prophets had yet taken
over only this one function of the old charismatics; the strategic
leadership itself is left to the king. This changed situation in contrast to the old wars is mirrored very vividly in this brief encounter
of Ahab with an anonymous prophet:

> And behold, a prophet came near to Ahab king of Israel and said,
> "Thus says the LORD, Have you seen all this great multitude?
> Behold, I will give it into your hand this day; [so that] you shall
> know that I am the LORD." And Ahab [asked], "By whom?" He

[again] said, "Thus says the LORD, By the servants of the governors of the districts [הַמְּדִינוֹת בְּנַעֲרֵי שָׂרֵי]." Then he [asked],
"Who shall begin the battle?" He answered, "You." (1 Kgs.
20:13-14)

Here, first of all, is a genuinely ancient kind of prophecy, which
in a specific situation addresses a king with very concrete instructions. The command is spoken in direct words of Yahweh and
proceeds completely in the terminology and conceptions of the old
idea of sacral war. However, the person responsible to carry out the
war is not a charismatic leader, but a royal civil servant with a
professional troop under his command.[8] What a mixture! Here three
originally distinct institutions are interlocked with each other: prophecy, kingship (with professional soldiers), and holy war. This division between the functions—summoning people to war through the
prophet and execution of the war through the king and his agents—
was now admittedly dangerous enough. Was it then thinkable that
the latter would really let the rule of its action be prescribed by the
former? Was it not inevitable that the royal-stately apparatus set in
motion by the prophet (in the best of cases!) ultimately would have
to go on functioning according to its own inherent rules? In fact,
this separation of functions already basically concealed within itself
the possibility for the heaviest of conflicts between kingship and
prophecy, and it is important that here already we see clearly the
real root of this conflict. It lies not in an exceptionally difficult
problem of "prophet and politics," but is rather simply rooted in the
fact that the prophets had become spokesmen for the old requirements of holy war. However, at first these conflicts were still of a
lighter nature.[9] This was likely connected with the strength of the
north Israelite kingship at the time and the weakness of the court
prophets in those days, who—if at all—could carry out their own
proper function only in an agreed dependence on king and state.

---

8. The שָׂרֵי הַמְּדִינוֹת, 1 Kgs. 20:14-15, 17, 19. In v. 19 they are differentiated
from the חַיִל.

9. Such a case of conflict is reported, for instance, in 1 Kgs. 20:25ff.

How strongly prophecy and holy war had grown together, however, is shown especially by the old cry,

"My father, my father! The chariots of Israel and its horsemen!" (2 Kgs. 2:12; 13:14)

It is natural to assume that this utterance did not originally belong in the history of the ascension of Elijah and that its military point presupposes as origin a much more special context of meaning; it would seem rather to fit the context of the Elisha account of 2 Kgs. 13:14ff. Yet it would be futile to ask about the origin of a saying that is obviously a standard quotation. In any case, it is a polemic expression, a very radical slogan, which concerns the most elementary question of the very existence of Israel. It must stem from circles representing a certain patriarchal opposition to the transformation of the waging of war by new techniques. Protection and help for Israel are guaranteed only by the prophet. To infer from אָבִי (אָב is a prophetic title of dignity), the saying stems directly from prophetic circles and betrays the high self-confidence of this movement (2 Kgs. 6:21). But what this still obscure utterance can permit us to conclude is at least that the prophecy of the ninth century was not thought of only as an instrument of some sort of instruction—whether it be in messages of judgment or of consolation—but it was rather thought of as the guarantor of the protection of Israel against threats from outside; thus, prophecy pushed with its guarantee exactly into the place where previously the institution of holy war stood.[10]

The step from the prophecy of the ninth century to that of the eighth century is a very great one. It is so great that some have even attempted to sever completely the connection between the *nabi* [of the previous century] and the writing prophets [of the latter].[11] The questions about the internal history of the prophetic movement, which are still open to a great extent, lie far beyond our present

10. Concerning this far-reaching displacement cf. Jepsen, 186.
11. Jepsen [perhaps 132-142].

investigation; they can, however, in our opinion be clarified only by an investigation and separation of the individual Yahweh traditions, of which the prophets had become bearers and speakers here and there. In this respect, only a very small sector out of the manifold messages of the prophets will enter here into our field of vision. We will single out texts from Isaiah which are connected with the two most serious threats to Jerusalem, that of the Syro-Ephraimite War in 734 and the threat of Sennacherib in 701. How—that is, in what terms—did Isaiah express Yahweh's relationship to these events? Is his message conditioned by tradition in any way?

The passage Isa. 7:1-9 is in form-critical perspective a remarkably complicated construction, even apart from the somewhat problematic relationship of v. 1 to the rest of the text. First of all, because of its narrative character it must be described as one of the prophet's stories; however, the narrative form here is only the outward framework around a prophetic dictum, whose two members can be separated from one another quite clearly as "word of warning" (vv. 4-6) and "promise" (vv. 7-9). In both members the nearly baroque form surprises us; in particular, the word of warning has become unusually broad by its dispersal in the prose. But the word of promise is also complex; in terms of substance and disposition we can distinguish three elements: (1) the "No" of Yahweh (v. 7); (2) the reasons (vv. 8-9a); (3) the application *ad hominem* (v. 9b). Since the material is very familiar, we can limit ourselves here to the most fundamental principles. The concise exposition shows the king carrying out a military inspection; he is active and at the same time fearful. In direct contrast, Isaiah says he should not fear and should do nothing:

> Behold! Be still and without fear; your heart should not despair.
> (Isa. 7:4)

The first imperative (הִשָּׁמֵר) is well understood as a general call to vigilance, but it is also already strongly negative—that is, it calls for restraint. However, when Isaiah now by the order of

Yahweh commands one to be still and not to fear, that can only mean that the prophet proclaims this war as a holy war for Yahweh. In this case special rules apply for all of those who stand on the side of Yahweh, and the most important—however, also the most difficult—is this command of passivity. Interpreters have long pointed to the following word from Isaiah, certainly spoken in a substantially later time, as fully identical in content:

> "In returning and rest you shall be saved;
>   in quietness and in trust shall be your strength."
> And you would not, but you said,
> "No! We shall speed upon horses" . . . (Isa. 30:15-16)

The sense of the imperfect verb in the divine word is hardly to be translated, with Martin Luther and others, as merely potential ("you would be saved"); even less is it an imperative ("Seek salvation!") as interpreted by Otto Procksch. Rather, Isaiah is pointing out where Jerusalem's help and deliverance in fact lie, regardless of whether they are currently being perceived or not. Once again the subject is the most fundamental political problem of existence, and once again the contradiction is a drastic one: strength—the word גְּבוּרָה declared in Isa. 30:15 means particularly military strength—does not depend upon horses, but on "keeping quiet." So Yahweh raises the question of confidence in its exclusive sense; בְּטְחָה is just another word for what Isa. 7:9 called הַאֲמִין. There is no need now for further proof to show that Isaiah in the crisis of the Syro-Ephraimite War, and occasionally at other times, updated the old orders of the holy war. To let Yahweh act, to entrust oneself to him and not to fear—these were actually the motifs that we encountered over and over again in the old narratives. The way that Isaiah views Yahweh's acting absolutely as excluding any human military co-participation now shows clearly that Isaiah is not really reviving the ancient conception after all, for at that time, as we have seen, that contradiction between divine and human action was not yet known. Rather, we see Isaiah quite exactly representing that conception which we found in various forms among the later novella writers. Also, for Isaiah the faith refers to the absolute miracle of Yahweh. Thus the parallel between the conception in Isa. 7 and the account of Exod. 14 is indeed impressive. We need only to remember the pro-grammatic speech of Moses calling people not to fear, but to be still (תַּחֲרִישׁוּן) and to hold themselves prepared for the help of Yahweh (Exod. 14:13b-14). Moreover, the speech about faith in Yahweh is here as well (Exod. 14:31). There is a particular con-nection here which admittedly cannot be explained in the sense of a literary dependency, but certainly also not only in the sense of a mere dependent relationship in the "history of ideas." There is here a clearly outlined stream of tradition which even in the rela-tively late prophets still breaks through with surprising strength and liveliness. On the other hand, the difference is obvious: there [Exodus], a narrator who is teaching in an edifying way; here, a prophet who in real distress wants to prepare the way for the miracle through his call to faith.

The circle binding Exod. 14 and Isa. 7 would close completely if there would also be found [in Isaiah] a counterpart to the element in the Moses speech which we have not yet drawn in for compari-son. Moses had commanded:

"Stand firm, and see the salvation of the LORD." (Exod. 14:13)

Now we draw in the text from Isa. 22, which according to unanimous judgment stems from the time after Sennacherib's with-drawal, and we content ourselves with one brief excerpt.

In that day you looked to the weapons of the House of the Forest, and you saw that the breaches of the city of David were many, and you collected the waters of the lower pool, and you counted the houses of Jerusalem, and you broke down the houses to fortify the wall. You made a reservoir between the two walls for the water of the old pool. But you did not look to him who did it, or have regard for him who planned it long ago. (Isa. 22:8b-11)

What all has happened in Jerusalem! But the one thing that was needed did not happen! What, though, does Isaiah understand by "looking to Yahweh"? Definitely we must assume that this expression sounds flat and general only to our ears, and that by it Isaiah intended something very special. A connection with the cultic term "to look at God" certainly does not come into question. That expression applies to Yahweh's action in history. But it also is still much too general, for in what sense can one "see" Yahweh in history? According to Isaiah, Yahweh is especially hidden in his historical deeds! That the expression "to look to Yahweh" has a quite precisely outlined meaning is demonstrated by a very similar text, of which all we know for sure is that it comes from the later period of Isaiah.[12]

> Woe to those who go down to Egypt for help
>   and rely on horses,
> who trust in chariots because they are many
>   and in horsemen because they are very strong,
> but do not look to the Holy One of Israel
>   or consult the LORD! . . .
>
> [But] the Egyptians are men, and not God;
>   and their horses are flesh, and not spirit. (Isa. 31:1, 3)

Again Jerusalem is in great danger; Sennacherib is maneuvering, perhaps already in Palestine. Again, on what was certainly a widely debated question—"What must be done?"—Isaiah stands fundamentally against all politics of armament and alliance. Here as well, instead of every false activity and every false confidence, he calls for "looking to Yahweh" and consulting Yahweh. To consult Yahweh in the distress of war was, however, more than simply obtaining an oracle about the outcome of the war; it was inquiring whether Yahweh would participate in the battle—indeed,

---

12. This saying belongs in the time of the revolutionary movement of Syrian and Palestinian states against Sennacherib which was supported by Egypt and by an Egyptian-Ethiopian army corps (at the earliest, 705; at the latest, the Battle of Elteke, 701).

whether Yahweh would lead it or not. "To look to Yahweh," then, means to prepare oneself in full expectancy for his coming and his deed. That alone was Jerusalem's responsibility: to expect Yahweh and to look toward his deed of deliverance.[13] Thus, Isaiah's conception of holy war corresponds also in this respect rather exactly to the portrayal of Exod. 14:13-14. But now the pophetic word proceeds with the entire set of concepts of holy war; it has, though, been somewhat distorted in its second half (Isa. 31:4-5), and in any case is restored again only through emendation.[14] The word contains salvation for Zion, but destruction for those who nurture a false confidence. Yahweh himself will arise and as in the old holy wars will come down to the battle:

> The LORD of hosts will come down
> to fight upon Mount Zion and upon its hill,
> [. . .] he will protect and deliver it,
> he will spare and rescue it. (Isa. 31:4b-5)[15]

This text is, therefore, very important to us because here we can again see with greater accuracy how Isaiah concretely pictured the deliverance of Jerusalem by Yahweh. Moreover, we see how, according to Isaiah, the same would have happened in the Syro-Ephraimite War had Ahab only believed.

---

13. How solidly the motif of standing up and looking expectantly for Yahweh's salvation belongs to this interpretation of holy war is shown by 2 Chr. 20:17 (see below, 129-130). In Isaiah the reproach of not having looked for the work of Yahweh and not having seen his deeds is raised yet a third time in Isa. 5:12. It is possible that the situation in which that text was spoken and which we can no longer determine was something similar to that of Isa. 22 and 31:1. Isa. 17:7 is hardly from Isaiah himself.

14. We must insist on the fact that Isa. 31:1-5 is a unity. Vv. 1-3 are a reproach and vv. 4-5 are a statement by God (though stylized in the third person). But the preterite understanding of וַיָּבֹא (v. 2) should not be maintained.

15. The twice repeated עַל in v. 4 can under no circumstances be understood in the sense of "contrary to," "against" (contrary to Procksch) [perhaps his *Jesaja I-XXXIX.* KAT (Leipzig: A. Deichert, 1930)]. "Zion is not Yahweh's booty, but his possession" [Bernhard Duhm, *Das Buch Jesaia.* HKAT (Göttingen: Vandenhoeck & Ruprecht, 1892), on Isa. 3:1].

Lastly, an additional word concerning v. 3, which is often cited, but not yet adequately interpreted. What does the observation mean in this context that the horses of Egypt are "flesh, and not spirit"? The concept of רוּחַ is known to have played a very minor role among the writing prophets before the Exile; the text of Isa. 31:3 is therefore especially prominent and must have a special meaning. That Isaiah is thinking about the "spiritual power of truth, purity and righteousness"—that is, that the opposition between flesh and spirit is ethical—is not credible.[16] But likewise, the interpretation of the opposition in a more speculative sense as dealing with the creaturely versus the incorruptible is much too general also, even without taking account of the fact that the opposition between temporal and eternal is very foreign to the argument of the prophet.[17] Since the entire passage is pervaded by the concept of holy war, רוּחַ must here mean the charisma. Indeed, we saw sufficiently what an important role belonged to charisma in the initiation and waging of the holy wars. This therefore is Isaiah's meaning: the Egyptians lack the charisma by which alone victory in such a war is certain. This aid, on which Judah relies, is weak (בָּשָׂר). But who is the bearer of this charisma? Isaiah does not anymore think of a charismatic leader like the ones who arose in the times of the judges, and even less is he thinking of Ahaz or Hezekiah. He himself, the prophet, is the charismatic, and with this self-consciousness Isaiah stands precisely in the tradition of the word of Elijah: "My father, my father! The chariots of Israel and its horsemen!" (2 Kgs. 2:12; 13:14).[18]

16. Walther Eichrodt, *Theology of the Old Testament* II. OTL (Philadelphia: Westminster, 1967), 57. Jepsen (25 n. 2) thinks about the "opposition of flesh and vitality."

17. Paul Volz, *Der Geist Gottes und die verwandten Erscheinungen im Alten Testament und im anschliessenden Judentum* (Tübingen: J. C. B. Mohr, 1910), 49. Wilhelm Gesenius, *Hebräisches und aramäisches Handwörterbuch über das Alte Testament,* rev. Frants Buhl (Leipzig: F. C. W. Vogel, 1915), 120; *A Hebrew and English Lexicon of the Old Testament,* ed. Francis Brown, Samuel R. Driver, and Charles A. Briggs (Oxford: Clarendon, 1907), 142.

18. Duhm (192) interprets very correctly the וְלֹא רוּחִי of Isa. 30:1 with "not

Thus—we summarize—it has become quite clear that the old tradition of the holy war once again had found a powerful speaker in Isaiah of the eighth century. It is therefore certainly inappropriate when Bernard Duhm comments with surprise that with his utterance in Isa. 30:15 the prophet "was centuries ahead of his time."[19] On the contrary, we see that in a rather anachronistic way Isaiah reaches back to the old faith tradition, the validity and binding forces of which his secularized contemporaries thought they had long since outgrown. Precisely so, this characteristic fits ideally into the picture we have of the prophets of the eighth century, for their primary task was actualizing the old patriarchal tradition that had long since ceased to be binding—as, for example, the old legal order. Thereby we have at the same time said that the body of traditions concerning the holy war naturally cannot be a universal key to interpreting Isaiah. Yet when times of foreign political and military threat give him occasion, the prophet always stands ready with his proclamation in its succession. On the other hand, precisely those thoughts which are held to be especially central and characteristic for Isaiah flowed to the prophet from this tradition.[20] From there he got the idea of faith, from there the rejection of armaments and alliances, and from there the motif of looking to Yahweh and of standing still. It is not too much to say that Isaiah sees the whole universal activity of Yahweh in history—the מַעֲשֵׂה יהוה—in the form of holy war, of a final eschatological mobilization and battle of Yahweh for Zion (Isa. 5:12, 19; 10:12). Thus, prophecies such as Isa. 17:12ff., concerning the chaotic attack in the defense of the peoples, or Isa. 9:4-5, concerning the final victory before the enthronement of the anointed one, lie directly within the realm of these thoughts. On the other hand, it is also clear how distant Isaiah stands with this updating from the old sacral-cultic world of the original holy wars. He stands much

---

with consultation of my prophet." [Editor's note: Duhm actually says "not with my Spirit, that is, under the consultation of my prophet."]

19. Duhm, on Isa. 30:15ff., 197.

20. Compare as well the allusions to the "day of Midian" in Isa. 9:4; 10:26.

nearer to the conception of those humanized and theologized narratives, especially the narrative of Exod. 14. Furthermore, Isaiah
rejects all military activity in holy war; indeed, he radicalizes the
tendency which already in those novellas had so obviously re-
pressed any human synergism. What is new with Isaiah, moreover,
is the fusion of that old tradition with his thoughts of the legitimacy
and the invulnerability of Zion which on their part stem from a
completely different stream of tradition—namely, the one which
was triggered by the prophecy of Nathan.[21]

*   *   *

It would hardly be fruitful if we sought now to register every
incidental allusion to the conception of holy war in the books of
the prophets. What would be gained if we were to find here and
there an echo, with a style which reflected clearly and with phe-
nomenal vividness the event and the customs from all realms of
life, the profane as well as the sacred? The question can only be
whether the message of other prophets is also in any way substantially conditioned by the complex of traditions of the holy war.
Just a superficial survey demonstrates immediately that no other
prophet stood even approximately so strongly in the shadow of
this tradition as did Isaiah. The reasons for this fact we cannot
adequately understand. Concerning Amos we could indeed say that
neither the outward history nor the themes of his own message
brought him into any kind of actual proximity to this traditional
sphere of ideas. Yet this explanation is hardly sufficient. Listen
only to the last proclamation of judgment in the strophe about
Israel in his poem concerning all the nations:

21. A thorough treatment of the question of holy war in Isaiah would amount
practically to a monograph about this prophet. Without claiming to exhaust the
additional material, we should still point to Isa. 30:27-33: Yahweh comes from afar,
his arm falls, he lets himself be seen, "a flame of devouring fire, with a cloudburst
and tempest and hailstones" fall on the people. The tradition-historical origins of
these elements of the concept need no further discussion. Isa. 19:1-3 describes the
"panic before God," which comes over Egypt and its gods at the advance of Yahweh.

"Flight shall perish from the swift,
    and the strong shall not retain his strength,
    nor shall the mighty save his life;
he who handles the bow shall not stand,
    and he who is swift of foot shall not save himself,
    nor shall he who rides the horse save his life;
and he who is stout of heart among the mighty
    shall flee away naked in that day," says the LORD.
                                        (Amos 2:14-16)

Ernst Sellin already recognized that here Amos is describing a "divine terror."[22] Indeed, we have here no doubt the most detailed description of this rare phenomenon: through some kind of an inexplicable blow from below, a mysterious immobilization befell the warrior through which all of the tried and tested arts of war were rendered inoperative. Thus Amos here—just as in 5:3—sees the judgment coming upon Israel in the form of a military catastrophe caused by Yahweh. It is perhaps too much to say that here Yahweh is turning against Israel in a holy war, for Amos utilizes just one motif out of the old traditional complex in order to dramatize his picture of judgment. But we must say that in such a perspective any kind of positive reappropriation of the conception of holy war was no longer possible for Amos.

It is different in Micah. It is not easy to separate the different units from one another in the second half of the fourth chapter. It is advisable, however, to take the relevant passage Mic. 4:11-13 to be a unity in itself:

Now many nations
    are assembled against you,
saying, "Let her be profaned,
    and let our eyes gaze upon Zion."
But they do not know
    the thoughts of the LORD,

22. Ernst Sellin, *Das Zwölfprophetenbuch*, 2nd ed. KAT 12/1: Hosea-Micha (Leipzig: A. Deichert, 1929): 209.

they do not understand his plan,
    that he has gathered them as sheaves to the threshing floor.
Arise and thresh,
    O daughter of Zion,
for I will make your horn iron
    and your hoofs bronze;
you shall beat in pieces many peoples,
    and shall devote[23] their gain to the LORD,
    their wealth to the Lord of the whole earth.

The passage is divided into two parts: in vv. 11-12 the prophet describes the end-time historical situation; in v. 13 in direct address Yahweh gives the signal for mobilization and military action. The question of the authenticity of the passage, which for us is certainly not of very great significance, cannot be decided against Micah on the grounds that one declares the passage to be an imitation of Ezek. 38–39.[24] The expectation of an almost apocalyptic attack by the nations against the city of God is a traditional eschatological construct that certainly already had a history behind itself at the times of Micah and Isaiah (cf. Isa. 8:9-10; 17:12ff.; 29:7). We could rather ask whether for Micah, in the light of his catastrophic words about Zion (Mic. 3:12), the city of God would still have such an eschatological significance. However, this exclusive argumentation from one passage against another is dangerous, for the prophets do not speak out of a systematic doctrinal whole, but rather they make relevant from case to case the most diverse eschatological traditions. And the word of the thoughts of Yahweh concerning history, in terms of his "council," leads us right into the immediate neighborhood of Isaiah. The content of the conclusion is of great unity and weight: the nations storm Zion, but they do not know that they have been gathered together there by Yahweh himself for their own destruction, for they will be trampled over

---

23. This translates הַחֲרַמְתְּ.
24. Emil Kautsch, "Micha," in *Kurzes Bibelwörterbuch,* ed. Hermann Guthe (Tübingen: J. C. B. Mohr, 1903), 434.

by Israel as sheaves by cattle. This picture of the threshing brings us to the intention of the final result. The booty will then be dedicated to Yahweh. Micah seems thus to expect the conquest of the world of the nations through an end-time holy war for which Yahweh gives the signal to begin and the power of victory. Thus we have here two sets of interrelated ideas. Prominent is that of the siege attack by the nations and the deliverance through Yahweh; woven into it, however, is the concept of an eschatological holy war.

From Mic. 4:11-13 a direct path leads us to Ezek. 38–39, for the prophecy concerning Gog and Magog is nothing but a baroque elaboration of that same complex of ideas regarding a siege attack of the chaotic masses of the nations and their repulse by Yahweh. This defense is carried out as follows:

> [Certainly] on that day there shall be a great shaking in the land of Israel; the fish of the sea, and the birds of the air, and the beasts of the field, and all creeping things that creep on the ground, and all the men that are upon the face of the earth, shall quake at my presence, and the mountains shall be thrown down, and the cliffs shall fall, and every wall shall tumble to the ground. I will summon every kind of terror against Gog, says the Lord GOD; every man's sword will be against his brother. With pestilence and bloodshed I will enter into judgment with him; and I will rain upon him and his hordes and the many peoples that are with him, torrential rains and hailstones, fire and brimstone . . . (Ezek. 38:19-22)[25]

Here nearly all of the traditional motifs of holy war are yet together: the divine terror, the earthquake, hail from heaven, and the murderous panic among the enemies. One might think that

---

25. The הָרַי חֶרֶב in v. 21 is certainly prescribed from חַרְבָּה (LXX). That Yahweh sends the sword above his mountain does not fit right and anticipates moreover the following "a sword through the other." The passage is emended according to the LXX by Alfred Bertholet, *Hesekiel.* HAT 13 (Tübingen: J. C. B. Mohr, 1936): 130; J. W. Rothstein; Hans Schmidt, *Die grossen Propheten.* SAT 2 (Göttingen: Vandenhoeck & Ruprecht, 1915): 445; and others.

Ezekiel had simply copied from 1 Sam. 14:15-20.[26] But the relationship may not be explained so simply or so literarily. We are dealing with motifs which for a long time have been traditionally dictated, which is demonstrated by a text in Haggai, who certainly did not copy from Ezek. 38:

> I am about to shake the heavens and the earth, and to overthrow the throne of kingdoms; I am about to destroy the strength of the kingdoms of the nations, and overthrow the chariots and their riders; and the horses and their riders shall go down, every one by the sword of his fellow. (Hag. 2:21-22)

This logion, of which only half has been cited here, overarches the entire message of this prophet with a sweeping messianic end-time vision. The traditional motif of the earthquake has been broadened out here into universal dimensions, as already in Ezekiel. Battle chariots, horses and riders—which have obviously gathered themselves together for a military procession against Israel—are annihilated, falling one at the sword of the other. Here, too, is discernible the idea of an eschatological holy war. Ezekiel and Haggai differ from Mic. 4 only in that they recognize no military participation of Israel. The catastrophe is carried out by the earthquake and the divine terror effected by Yahweh alone.

We find similar themes in Zechariah as well. When the prophet demands the renunciation of all kinds of fortification during the time when certainly everyone in Jerusalem was discussing the question of building the wall, when he proclaims that Yahweh alone will protect the new Jerusalem, that is easily recognizable as the most central motif of the concept of holy war. Here the old slogan "not armaments, but Yahweh" has admittedly undergone a metamorphosis, but Isaiah had already programmatically carried out its application to the *polis*. What is new here is the extreme eschatologizing. When Yahweh himself as a wall of fire defends the city of God and is present in it in his *doxa*, that means the

26. See above, 48-49.

breaking off of all previous relations and the breaking in of the final and definitive reality. That such traditions are vivid in Zechariah is shown ever much more pointedly by the following logion which, with others, through some kind of very disruptive misfortune interrupts the context of the vision of the lamps:

> "This is the word of the LORD to Zerubbabel: Not by might, nor by power, but by my Spirit, says the LORD of hosts." (Zech. 4:6)

On grounds of both form and content this utterance must, without question, be taken alone. It obviously has nothing to do with the matter of building the temple; it seems much rather to refer to the question of the establishment of a military power—a question which very likely would have arisen in the process of the reconstruction of the whole community, which must have been still very weak and defeated.[27] The logion would then be understood as a "word for discussion," and it would stand objectively in tight connection with the question of building the wall, for a wall must ultimately also be defended. Thereby we have seen how to interpret it: the contrast between חַיִל and רוּחַ [here in Zech. 4] is the same as the contrast between בָּשָׂר and רוּחַ in Isa. 31:3. Everything must be entrusted to Yahweh and his initiative and his empowerment. Charisma, not human security!

Zech. 4:6 resonantly concludes the series of utterances in which prophets pick up and make relevant the old traditions of holy war; and we see that the old tradition was still able to rise up with concentrated power even in the late Zechariah. If we look back at the instances cited, we see immediately that in them we are dealing neither with reference to the real life of the people nor with an effective institution, as for instance with the institution of the tribunal or the sacrificial worship cult which still functioned concretely in full view of the prophet. What we found briefly treated here in the prophet's words were elements of tradition

---

27. Friedrich Horst, *Die zwölf Kleinen Propheten,* 2nd ed. HAT 14/2: *Nahum bis Maleachi* (Tübingen: J. C. B. Mohr, 1954), 232.

which after the cessation of the institution became constitutive elements of faith in Yahweh, of which the binding force and undiminished validity were admittedly seriously doubted by the secularized contemporaries of the prophets. Incidentally as well, the entire set of ideas about holy war is never renewed by the prophets; the connection to the cultic-sacral sphere is completely abandoned. None of the offerings or rites is mentioned anymore as a demand for the prophets' audience. The reappropriation of these traditions by the prophets is limited much more to the strongly spiritualized central motif of believing in the self-sufficiency of Yahweh's help over against all human busy-ness. It must furthermore be said that in the entirety of the prophetic proclamation the holy war is no longer absolutely the only form of Yahweh's help for Israel; rather, it stands as only one more possibility among others of divine saving activity. Nevertheless, the polemical word about the prophet who represents Israel's riders and chariots shows that prophecy was conscious of itself almost as the rightful successor to the old institution of holy war, or at least as the executor of the legacy of that tradition, and had acted accordingly. Indeed, the displacement is such that now the prophet with his charisma virtually steps into the position held by self-defense through armed might. In general, we must designate in Isaiah the spiritualized idea of holy war as the one focal point of his entire prophecy, beside which the hope of David-Zion stands as the other. What still remains temporarily unexplained is the question of how the old tradition can have stood so much in the center for this one prophet, whereas other prophets seem not to know it.

CHAPTER 5
_____

Deuteronomy and Holy War

THE BOOK OF DEUTERONOMY is in the whole Old Testament by far
the richest source concerning the concepts and customs of holy
war. As a single body of texts it not only contains a series of
detailed normative orders and prescriptions about the behavior and
customs in the camp, before the battle, and so forth, but also in
striking contrast to the holiness law or the book of the covenant
it is thoroughly saturated from the first to the last chapter by an
outspoken war ideology, the origins and theological content of
which cannot help becoming a problem to us. All of the addresses
and laws in Deuteronomy are issued to an Israel which is constantly conscious of its enemies; this steadfast gaze at the enemies,
at "the nations," over against which Israel must and will affirm its
claims, is the most dominant characteristic of Deuteronomy.

> 6:18: ". . . And you shall do what is right and good in the
> sight of the LORD . . . that you may go in and take pos-
> session of the good land . . . by thrusting out all your
> enemies from before you, as the LORD has promised."
> 7:1-2: "When the LORD your God brings you into the land
> which you are entering to take possession of it, and clears
> away many nations before you . . . and when the LORD
> your God gives them over to you, and you defeat them;
> then you must utterly destroy them."
> 11:22ff.: "For if you will be careful to do all this command-
> ment . . . then the LORD will drive out all these nations before

115

you, and you will dispossess nations greater and mightier than yourselves. . . . No man shall be able to stand against you; the LORD your God will lay the fear of you and the dread of you upon all the land that you shall tread . . ."

12:29: "When the LORD your God cuts off before you the nations whom you go in to dispossess, and you dispossess them and dwell in their land . . ."

19:1: "When the LORD your God cuts off the nations whose land the LORD your God gives you, and you dispossess them . . ."

20:16-17: "But in the cities of these peoples that the LORD your God gives you for an inheritance, you shall save alive nothing that breathes, but you shall utterly destroy them . . ."

From Deuteronomy therefore came that war ideology which through the Deuteronomistic editing of many historic books— virtually the entire Old Testament—contributed that additional element of militant spirit and programmatic irreconcilability which has so frequently alienated people.

It is well known that the author of Deuteronomy drew into his body of texts all kinds of legal material which derives from considerably older times and that, as a result, visible tensions occasionally arose between this older legal material and the author's own conceptions and intentions. Furthermore, it can be held as demonstrated that the old narrative traditions of the author of Deuteronomy are presented in a pronounced parenetic style and homiletic loosening.[1] The law about the camp demonstrates how much we are actually dealing with preached law.

9. "When you go forth against your enemies and are in camp, then you shall keep yourself from every evil thing. 10. If there is among you any man who is not clean by reason of what chances to him by night, then . . . 12. You shall have a place outside the

1. Gerhard von Rad, *Studies in Deuteronomy.* Studies in Biblical Theology 9 (London: SCM and Chicago: Henry Regnery, 1953): 11-24.

camp and you shall go out to it. . . . 14. Because the LORD your
God walks in the midst of your camp (הִתְהַלֵּךְ), to save you and
to give up your enemies before you, therefore your camp must
be holy, that he may not see anything indecent among you, and
turn away from you. (Deut. 23:9-14)

The old tradition material lies obviously in 23:10-13; however,
now that has been circumscribed by common parenesis in vv. 9
and 14. It is remarkable that the old material obviously needs such
a parenetic interpretation like the one it is given in v. 14. Here the
text is speaking to a time which no longer takes as self-evident
that it is bound to such orders, but which must first be led to such
an understanding. Incidentally, it is odd that the author of Deuteronomy, who so consistently accentuates Yahweh's dwelling in
heaven[2] that he not once ventures to speak of a personal presence
of Yahweh at the cultic place, does speak here of Yahweh entering
into the camp. We must say that here the weight of the old,
handed-down conception pushed the author somewhat away from
his own theological course.

In the law about the siege of cities (Deut. 20:10-18, 19-20),
on the other hand, what has been preserved can hardly be an actual
old order of holy war, for it is very hard to imagine that in the
course of the old holy war there was ever a case of besieging a
city with proper siege techniques.[3] In any case, a very humane
inclination and, in particular, the initial offer of peace (v. 10)
contradict completely the spirit of the old wars. Finally, the imitator
betrays himself in the rationalized motivation given for the command of ḥērem: the inhabitants of the Canaanite cities are to be
destroyed "that they may not teach you to emulate (RSV "do
according to") all their abominable practices" (v. 18). Again we
see that an old rite requires an interpretation. Here the author of
Deuteronomy introduces a thought that was totally foreign to the

2. Deut. 26:15; 1 Kgs. 8:30, 32, 34, 36, 39, 43, 45, 49. Compare especially
Deut. 4:36 with Exod. 19:11, 18, 20.
3. V. 20 thinks of siege machines; cf. the annals report in 2 Chr. 26:15.

earlier Israelites. We saw that the old holy wars were waged simply
for the defensive protection of the physical existence of the
Yahweh amphictyony and that they were not at all directed against
the worship or beliefs of the enemies.[4] That is now decisively
changed when the author conceives of the holy wars as predominantly wars of religion, in which Israel turns offensively against
the Canaanite cult which is irreconcilable with faith in Yahweh.

1. "When you go forth to war against your enemies, and see horses
and chariots and an army larger than your own, you shall not be
afraid of them; for the LORD your God is with you, who brought
you up out of the land of Egypt. 2. *And when you draw near to
the battle, the priest shall come forward and speak to the people,*
3. *and shall say to them, 'Hear, O Israel, you draw near this day
to battle against your enemies; let not your heart faint; do not fear,
or tremble, or be in dread of them;* 4. *for the LORD your God is he
that goes with you, to fight for you against your enemies, to give
you the victory.'* 5. Then the officers shall speak to the people,
saying, 'What man is there that has built a new house and has not
dedicated it? Let him go back to his house, lest he die in the battle
and another man dedicate it. 6. And what man is there that has
planted a vineyard and has not enjoyed its fruit? Let him go back
to his house, lest he die in the battle and another man enjoy its
fruit. 7. And what man is there that has betrothed a wife and has
not taken her? Let him go back to his house, lest he die in the battle
and another man take her.' 8. *And the officers shall speak further
to the people, and say, 'What man is there that is fearful and
fainthearted? Let him go back to his house, lest the heart of his
fellows melt as his heart.'* 9. And when the officers have made an
end of speaking to the people, then commanders shall be appointed
at the head of the people. (Deut. 20:1-9)

Clarity reigns with respect to the literary composition of this
decree.[5] Obviously the statement of the priest styled in the plural

4. See above, 72-73.
5. Carl Steuernagel, *Das Deuteronomium*, 2nd ed. HKAT 3/1 (Göttingen:
Vandenhoeck & Ruprecht, 1923): 126-27.

in 20:2-4 is a secondary intrusion. However, the exclusion of the cowards by the officials in v. 8 also looks very much like an addition since it is introduced once again as a new address of the officials to the army (v. 8a). Thus we have in this text, first of all, a typical example of the way in which the author of Deuteronomy makes old orders relevant by placing them within a parenetic context (v. 1). The work of comparative history of religions has first of all demonstrated that an actual ancient custom is present within the speech of the officials.[6] This address is concerned in an entirely practical way with purely objective ritual things; it especially lacks the characteristic Deuteronomic touch—that subjective turn, that tendency toward internalization, and those efforts to make the cultic and ritual dimension understandable by means of interpretation. Therein especially, and not only by virtue of the above-named formal criteria, v. 8 betrays itself as typically Deuteronomic, for it supplements the address of the officials by means of a question about the subjective spiritual disposition of the warriors. Furthermore, it gives a reasonable explanation for why the elimination of those who have no courage is necessary. That this rationalizing reference to the danger of contagion by the presence of the disheartened does not at all meet the old meaning of the rituals is an observation that can be made at each step in all the interpretations of older cultic practices in Deuteronomy.[7]

Therefore, in all of its layers the text deals with holy war; the inserted priestly address, thus the most recent portion, differs from the older traditional material only in that it reflects upon the entirety of the imminent military event and wants to make the hearers fully aware. The question is now whether with the priestly declaration of war commanded in vv. 2-4 we are dealing with a purely

---

6. Friedrich Schwally, *Semitische Kriegsaltertümer,* 1:75-99. Those of the older period naturally did not know the institution of the "officers" (שֹׁטְרִים). They were a royal authority, and the recruitment of the general levy was incumbent upon them. Erhard Junge, *Der Wiederaufbau des Heerwesens,* 48-52.

7. His lack of courage in the first place makes him displeasing to the deity. Cf. the earlier shift in the meaning of the command of *ḥērem* above, 117.

literary fiction or, instead, whether an actually practiced custom stands behind this order. The literary evidence seems not to be favorable to the latter hypothesis. Meanwhile, we should ask whether something that is literarily secondary must also have had in real history a secondary or problematic existence. We should really separate literary-critical judgments from form-critical judgments anyway, since even behind late and decidedly theorizing texts actually practiced cultic customs can come to light.[8]

The priestly declaration of war in Deut. 20:2-4 does not stand alone in Deuteronomy either in its content or in its form. In the parenetic preface of Deut. 6–11 there are several passages which closely coincide with this text.

"And you shall destroy all the peoples that the LORD your God will give over to you, your eye shall not pity them; neither shall you serve their gods, for that would be a snare to you.

"If you say in your heart, 'These nations are greater than I; how can I dispossess them?' you shall not be afraid of them, but you shall remember what the LORD your God did to Pharaoh and to all Egypt, the great trials which your eyes saw, the signs, the wonders, the mighty hand, and the outstretched arm, by which the LORD your God brought you out; so will the LORD your God do to all the peoples of whom you are afraid. Moreover the LORD your God will send hornets among them, until those who are left and hide themselves from you are destroyed. You shall not be in dread of them; for the LORD your God is in the midst of you, a great and terrible God. The LORD your God will clear away these nations before you little by little; you may not make an end of them at once, lest the wild beasts grow too numerous for you. But the LORD your God will give them over to you, and throw them into great confusion [panic] (וְהָמָם מְהוּמָה), until they are destroyed. And he will give their kings into your hand, and you shall make their name perish from under heaven; not a man shall be able to stand against you, until you have destroyed them. The graven images of their gods you shall burn with fire; you shall not covet the silver or the gold that is on them, or take it for yourselves, lest you be ensnared by it; for it is an abomination to the LORD your God. And you shall not bring an abominable thing into your house, and become accursed like it (וְהָיִיתָ חֵרֶם); you shall utterly detest and abhor it; for it is an accursed thing. (Deut. 7:16-26)

The form-critical analysis—not yet fully carried through—has up to the present traced small sermonlike units in the parenetic preface of Deuteronomy—more exactly, parenetic speeches of the Levites which framed the reading of the law as admonitory speeches and as promises of blessings.[9] The passage before us here refuses, however, to fit into this form-critical category. It is a unity in itself. It was preceded by a promise of blessing (Deut. 7:12-15), and it is followed by a new word of admonition (8:1ff.). But while we recognize in those texts which frame it just that kind of preaching of the law, there is missing completely in 7:16-26 any allusion to Yahweh's desire for justice or to the law, "which I command you this day." Even more one-sidedly, here the faith principles of the holy war are reported. Do not fear—Yahweh fights—he brings a divine terror upon the enemies—stay away from the banned! Is not the conceptual range of the holy war rather completely traversed in this speech? If the *Sitz im Leben* of this parenetic section may at all be questioned, all that it can be is a speech [addressed to people] in a holy war. And yet—even if we can posit this usage already at such an early time—it cannot possibly have been spoken this way in the time of the judges. When we presuppose here a problem on the part of the listeners to which the text can speak pastorally (v. 17) and when the faith

9. August Klostermann, *Der Pentateuch: Beiträge zu seinem Verständnis und seiner Enstchungsgeschichte,* 2nd ser. (Leipzig: A. Deichert, 1907), 348; Ludwig Köhler, *Die hebräische Rechtsgemeinde.* Jahresbericht des Universität Zürich, 1930/31, 17ff.; Gerhard von Rad, *The Problem of the Hexateuch and Other Essays* (1966; repr. London: SCM and Philadelphia: Fortress, 1984), 26-33.

is then called upon to strengthen oneself indirectly through re-
membrance of the events of history, that betrays clearly the spirituality of a relatively late time. Furthermore, the exhortation to
allow no room for sympathy in this particular case (v. 16) would
presumably have been superfluous in the earlier time.

> "Hear, O Israel; you are to pass over the Jordan this day, to go
> in to dispossess nations greater and mightier than yourselves,
> cities great and fortified up to heaven, a people great and tall,
> the sons of the Anakim, whom you know, and of whom you have
> heard it said, 'Who can stand before the sons of Anak?' Know
> therefore this day that he who goes over before you as a devour-
> ing fire is the LORD your God; he will destroy them and subdue
> them before you; so you shall drive them out, and make them
> perish quickly, as the LORD has promised you.
>
> "Do not say in your heart, after the LORD your God has thrust
> them out before you, 'It is because of my righteousness that the
> LORD has brought me in to possess this land'; whereas it is
> because of the wickedness of these nations that the LORD is
> driving them out before you. Not because of your righteousness
> or the uprightness of your heart are you going in to possess their
> land; but because of the wickedness of these nations the LORD
> your God is driving them out from before you, and that he may
> confirm the word which the LORD swore to your fathers, to
> Abraham, to Isaac, and to Jacob.
>
> "Know therefore that the LORD your God is not giving you
> this good land to possess because of your righteousness; for you
> are a stubborn people." (Deut. 9:1-6)

The observations which we made regarding the previous text
also fit for this one. The law given by Moses, the question of
obedience, and the promise of blessing in the case of obedience
lie completely outside the field of vision. Rather, this text functions
completely within the ideology of the holy war. However, what
moves us nevertheless to consider such thoughts as not being "old"
is valid here possibly to an even greater degree. The warning
against self praise shows that the speaker is reckoning throughout

with the possibility of a very secular understanding of the events of war. It is characteristic also that behind the entire reflection stands a desire for understanding—namely, the question about the reason for the expulsion of the Canaanites ("not for the sake of your merit, but because of their malice").

> "The LORD your God himself will go over before you; he will destroy these nations before you, so that you shall dispossess them; and Joshua will go over at your head, as the LORD has spoken. And the LORD will do to them as he did to Sihon and Og, the kings of the Amorites, and to their land, when he destroyed them. And the LORD will give them over to you, and you shall do to them according to all the commandment which I have commanded you. Be strong and of good courage; do not fear or be in dread of them; for it is the LORD your God who goes with you; he will not fail you or forsake you."
>
> Then Moses summoned Joshua, and said to him in the sight of all Israel, "Be strong and of good courage; for you shall go with this people into the land which the LORD has sworn to their fathers to give them; and you shall put them in possession of it. It is the LORD who goes before you; he will be with you, he will not fail you or forsake you; do not fear or be dismayed." (Deut. 31:3-6, 7-8)

Nothing more needs to be said about the similarity between these two brief texts and those cited before. The hypothesis that here we are concerned with only a purely literary work of the author of Deuteronomy is not sufficient to explain adequately these texts which turn up time after time in the most diverse contexts. In our opinion we have to consider them as "formulae" of addresses, as examples of a *Gattung*. That is, a particular *Sitz im Leben* must have created the form and the phraseology appropriate to the situation. The question is now whether in the time of the author of Deuteronomy such practices, even such a restoration of the patterns of the holy war at all, can be made probable.

To answer this question, we must briefly take up again the

matters of historical-political events and the nature of the army. That the development in both kingdoms had to proceed first of all along the line of an ever-broader extension of the use of professional warriors and fortifications—that is, in the sense of a growing technologizing of the military under the repression of the old militia—would also be something that we should hypothesize if it were not substantiated by various pieces of evidence in the sources.[10] In the southern kingdom, Rehoboam, Asa, Amaziah, and Uzziah—to name only the most important—were deeply concerned for fortification. Even the construction of catapults by Uzziah is credibly reported (2 Chr. 26:15). If we think of the armament of those fortresses, we have a very dramatic commentary on Isaiah's complaint, "Their [Judah's] land is filled with horses, and there is no end to their chariots" (Isa. 2:7). However, Isaiah had at that time experienced the great catastrophe of 701. Jerusalem had capitulated, and the larger part of the kingdom of Judah was assigned by Sennacherib to his Philistine vassals.[11] That the mercenaries with their horses and chariots were taken away by Assyria and incorporated into its army can be presupposed as certain.[12] The weight of this catastrophe is obvious; indeed, by it nothing less than the entire development which the military had undergone since David and Solomon was now liquidated with one blow. Nevertheless, after a relatively brief time we see Judah under Josiah fully armed again and as a major military power on the horizon. How was that possible? The work of Erhard Junge, which we have cited several times, attempted to answer this question. That the land, having been bled, could now with its empty treasury

10. 2 Chr. 11:5b-10a; 1 Kgs. 15:16-22; 2 Kgs. 14:22; 2 Chr. 26:9, 15a. Concerning the literary assessment, of which we might take specimen copies from Chronicles, cf. Martin Noth, *Überlieferungsgeschichtliche Studien.* 3rd ed. Schriften der Königsberger Gelehrten Gesellschaft 18/2 (Tübingen: Max Niemeyer, 1967): 140-41.

11. Wilhelm Rudolph, "Sanherib in Palästina," *PJ* 25 (1929): 59-80. Albrecht Alt, "Nachwort über die territorialgeschichtliche Bedeutung von Sanheribs Eingriff in Palästina," *PJ* 25 (1929): 80-88.

12. For examples of this practice by the Assyrians, see Junge, 25.

establish a new mercenary army capable of fighting is hardly thinkable; there are no grounds for such an idea in the sources.

> Then no doubt there must have been really only one single alternative in spite of the lack in financial means to build a new *Wehrmacht* for the kingdom of Judah—namely, without recruiting or buying from the outside, but to build it out of what the land itself offered. That meant that the able-bodied men of the land would have to be enlisted for military service. This could be demanded of every subject of the empire as an obligation to the state, and thereby it would be possible to form a sufficiently strong, yet not too expensive army. In other words, the old militia system which had been long forgotten had to be awakened to new life.[13]

The result of this thesis, which can be considered as proven, gives us precisely the missing piece to close the circle. Indeed, the institution of the holy war was, as we have seen, especially an affair of the militia, and through the repression of the militia it had undergone progressive disintegration. What could be more natural than that together with the renewal of the militia to its old military dignity the old conception of the real essence and meaning of the wars of Israel could also arise again.[14] The agricultural circles from which the militia was recruited were, of course, still much more bound to patriarchal faith and patriarchal customs than the circles around the court, the officials, and the professional officers in the capital, who previously made all the political and military decisions. As the old tribe and clan associations became active, other religious forces also suddenly moved into the center—religious forces which for centuries had been excluded or strongly pushed to the periphery by the predominance of the capital. The question of cause and effect, though, is not easy to answer when interpreting this process of a drastic inner shift of emphasis.

13. Junge, 29.
14. The old militia was never completely liquidated; for instance, 2 Kgs. 15:20 speaks of people liable for service.

It would be conceivable that this patriarchal element first became such an important factor in the process of a military reform—that is, that it took place more mediately. More likely, however, is the assumption that the עַם הָאָרֶץ, the free rural population, especially after the catastrophe of 701, pursued a planned national politics and seized political decisions of far-reaching consequences.[15] So it does not seem possible to us to interpret the entire book of Deuteronomy otherwise than in a close connection with this patriarchal restoration movement. The agricultural bearers of this movement were still orthodox in the sense of the old conscription of the Yahweh amphictyony—or, rather, they believed that they were. Evidently the set of ideas about holy war formed a principal enzyme of their faith; indeed, if we may see in Deuteronomy a faithful expression of their thoughts and their desires, then we could say that their idea of holy war was the actual core of all of their thinking about Israel around which everything else could be organically grouped. Then this is after all the fiction of the book of Deuteronomy: it is a speech addressed to troops who with weapon in hand await great godly deeds of liberation. Obviously the time of Josiah received its great political and military impetus from this movement. That—admittedly in accordance with the fate of all restoration movements—the Deuteronomic restoration could actually rediscover the old reality only in somewhat broken forms and that the spirituality and the changed outward circumstances of the new time had still tacitly made their claims are both demonstrated by the inner tension which characterizes the entire book of Deuteronomy and which could already be made clear from the interpretation of the Deuteronomic laws of war and war speeches. The ideology of the holy war is here by no means a self-evident reality to which the army subordinates itself; rather, the army will be made aware through the full force of a convincing speech to the troops. Even this theologizing interpretation as such,

15. Indeed, Josiah himself had come to the throne through the intervention of the עַם הָאָרֶם (2 Kgs. 21:24). Von Rad, *Studies in Deuteronomy,* 65-66.

which wants so passionately to be committed to what is old, is also at those points where its rationalizing argumentation is not totally off the mark the most prominent sign of the far-reaching transformation that henceforth determined the spiritual complexion of this epoch.

CHAPTER 6

Conclusion and Prospect

WITH THE CATASTROPHIC DEFEAT of Josiah the institution of holy war in ancient Israel found its end. We have seen how it had become shattered already once earlier—namely, through the modified ways of waging war in the time of the kings—but that the time of the outward dissolution became at the same time the age of the most brilliant literary shaping of the ideology of holy war in the novellas after Solomon. After the thought-world of the holy war had already fully developed very independently in the prophetic movement, it then returned surprisingly under Josiah to its original institutional *Sitz im Leben* and from that setting once again gained new power and impetus. And now the event repeats itself, for after the destruction not only of the institution itself but of all military forces in general in the catastrophes of 608, 596, and 587 there ensues again a powerful literary sowing of a new seed, this time in a theological form—namely, in the Deuteronomic and Deuteronomistic reworking of the literature and in the historical narrative of the Chronicler.[1] This remarkable course could prompt some fundamental thinking. That such a cultic complex of traditions could after a certain time open itself to a strong spiritualization and then, in this process of transition, could reach far beyond its original cultic institutional restrictions is no doubt a rather

1. The Chronicler's historical account also stands fully in the tradition of the Deuteronomistic theology. Gerhard von Rad, *Das Geschichtsbild des chronistischen Werkes.* BWANT 54 [4/3] (Stuttgart: Kohlhammer, 1930): 54.

128

frequent, although not a regular, occurrence. However, our example shows especially that this process of spiritualization is not to be understood as a detachment and resumption of the older cultic and sacral understanding, on a higher level, so to speak. It does not take place, as it were, at the expense of the older; but it is rather the case that what we encounter in this spiritualized form are only fragments which loosed themselves from the matrix of the old institution and are given over to spiritualization, without the institution itself actually ceasing to exist as such—although for a long time it was scarcely observed. The institution was still there and after a long quiescence could even function again. Obviously, we can no longer understand the spiritualizing of the old cult ideas—and this important process has not yet been scrutinized—as a polemic reinterpretation and distancing from the cultically defined basis. The spiritualizing process is often nothing more than a free intellectual toying with isolated ideas, which took place at a certain stage of maturity, so to speak, above the cultic foundation without seriously calling into question its legitimacy.

We must, therefore, free ourselves from the assumption that there was a more or less hidden "polemic" or a taking up of a front and a principled distancing over against the world of the cult and its connections, so that we can take better account of the spiritualization of the holy war in the postexilic period. To conclude our study we choose two examples which in very different ways demonstrate the survival of the old motif.

1. In the account of the *war of Jehoshaphat against the peoples of the east* (2 Chr. 20:1-30), the old elements return again virtually in paradigmatic completeness, but in what spiritual sublimation! Martin Noth has suggested plausibly as the historical nucleus of the account an attack of a band of Nabateans in the pastoral area of the Judean villages south of Bethlehem;[2] out of this event the narrator constructs a threat in which the very existence or nonex-

2. "Eine palästinische Lokalüberlieferung in 2. Chr. 20," *ZDPV* 67 (1944/45): 46ff.

istence of the state of Judah was at stake. However, the king does not take arms, but in a service of fasting calls on Yahweh's help through an appeal to the salvation history (vv. 4-13). An inspired Levite commands the Judeans not to fear; the battle is not theirs, but Yahweh's (vv. 14-17). Before the battle the king gives a war sermon in which he admonishes the army to have faith (v. 20). Then the singers in their holy vestments are ranked in front of the battle array of the armed soldiers. As they have just begun with their song of praise, something "lying in wait" (מְאָרְבִים), thus some kind of supernatural powers, falls upon the enemy, who kill themselves reciprocally in the panic which ensues, so that the Judeans do not need to wield a sword.[3] There is nothing reported of a ḥērem; instead of this there is an additional thanksgiving celebration held at the location of the victory. However, a divine terror had fallen over the enemies of Judah. This account forms to an extent the culmination of the development of the conception of the holy war as absolute miracle, a path of development which had begun in the post-Solomonic humanism and had been represented in greater form by Isaiah. The inner connection with one of those earlier accounts is plain enough in the verbatim quotation from Exod. 14 ("stand still, and see . . . ," 2 Chr. 20:17) and the link with Isaiah in the citing of his word ("If you will not believe, surely you shall not be established" from Isa. 7, in 2 Chr. 20:20); and yet how strongly has the entire concept changed. The cultic dimension, the complete shedding of which surprised us, has now again become the most striking feature of the whole business, by means of the accent upon the various worshiplike observances. Meanwhile, the great clarity and transparency with which in prayer and preaching the concern for the dimension of faith is pressed upon people's consciousness is very different from the ancient attitude, but is the result of long and mature theological reflection. First of all, however, we are struck by the major role which now is incumbent upon the cult personnel. The characteristic of the old

3. To this intervention of heavenly powers compare 2 Chr. 14:12.

holy wars had been that they were carried on with a minimum of conspicuous officers. Here, on the other hand, a great apparatus of cult officials functioned, and great emphasis is placed upon the fact that the divine help is linked precisely with the initiation of their cultic activity.[4] How the old original war cry (תְּרוּעָה) has now been converted into a hymn of praise of an official group of the cultic personnel is shown especially clearly by the spiritualizing and leviticizing of the old body of ideas.

2. If we were to ascertain the elements of the concept of holy war which have merged into *the Psalms,* we would once again gain an impression of the wealth of elements which originally found their source in this particular cultic institution and have been scattered in all of the realms and activities of religious life. The oldest psalms are more recent than the latest holy wars. So in all of the texts which could be consulted here, we are dealing with the afterlife of the old motifs, with transposition into new situations or simply only with stereotyped reminiscences in the language of prayer out of a body of traditions which had become canonical. And yet it must be said that in the powerful מִלְחָמָה יהוה עִזּוּז וְגִבּוֹר יהוה גִּבּוֹר (Ps. 24:8) the archaic element is yet undiminished and echoes in glorious power. That in the *Gattung* of the royal psalms (cf. Pss. 18, 20, 21, 144) and especially of the communal laments (Pss. 44, 60) the old motifs were given particular attention needs no explanation. However, if we look at the historical reminiscences—that is, at the epic portrayals of salvation history—or even at the brief allusions to the past, we are struck by the fact that for them the time of the great military deeds of Yahweh is the time of the wandering in the desert and the Conquest, while the time of the judges—that is, the time of the actual holy wars—is insignificant in comparison.[5] So strongly is the historical reality

4. The shift of interest to the cultic officials is shown also in the word of Jehoshaphat, ". . . Believe his (levitical) prophets!" 2 Chr. 20:20.

5. Cf. Pss. 105, 135; Exod. 15. How briefly and simply Ps. 78, which otherwise is so long and boring, handles the time of the judges (vv. 56-60)! Likewise, Neh. 9:6-36 has practically nothing to say about the judges.

covered over by the canonical tradition which has become pre-
dominant! And the psalms of all of the *Gattungen* are based on
only the latter.

One small group of statements however still deserves special
attention:

> A king is not saved by his great army;
>> a warrior is not delivered by his great strength.
> The war horse is a vain hope for victory,
>> and by its great might it cannot save.
> Behold, the eye of the LORD is on those who fear him,
>> on those who hope in his steadfast love. (Ps. 33:16-18)

> His delight is not in the strength of the horse,
>> nor his pleasure in the legs of a man;
> but the LORD takes pleasure in those who fear him,
>> in those who hope in his steadfast love. (Ps. 147:10-11)

Both psalms are hymns, and both are certainly postexilic, perhaps even late postexilic. Moreover, it goes without saying that in
these psalm texts there survives a tradition which we know from
Isaiah, which in fact reaches back into the times when the Israelite
militia saw themselves opposed to the [technologically] superior
Canaanite war chariots. However, the far-reaching change which has
taken place is just as clear. For here horses, military power, and the
hero armed for battle are no longer concrete entities at all, no longer
a real political and strategic possibility. The psalmist does not at all
share anymore in the situation in which Isaiah found himself, where
the false trust in military armament and horses was a very real
political possibility, in favor of which Judah and its king had opted.
In both psalms the word about the horses is nothing more than an
image; it deals with a teaching of the faith brought into view by
means of the canonical, conventional idea of the warriors and horses
and thus in a way lifted up as a symbol for the human being who
depends on his own powers. We see that immediately in the antithesis
which these psalms formulate: not in horses and armor, but in those

who fear God does Yahweh have pleasure—that is, in the "quiet people in the land." Thus, what is at stake here is not the political problem of the existence and preservation of Israel among the nations, but individual piety—that is, a particular personal ideal of devoutness which expresses itself in the old motifs which have now become images. Here the ancient religious conceptions of holy war—which for the longest time had been connected to the collectivity of the people—have now finally reached the individual, to shape as well that individual's very personal faith in the trials of life.[6] Thereby, in our opinion, is indicated the longest road that the old set of ideas could possibly have traversed. Both songs referred to above are hymns—that is, their *Sitz im Leben* is postexilic congregational worship. Thus it is also the case here, as we determined it to be in 2 Chr. 20, that the tradition of holy war after many turns in the road has found its way back again into the traditional worship of Yahweh from which it first emerged.

In the era of the Maccabees the Jews unexpectedly intervened once again in the political events with weapons, and, as we may believe in the reporting of the first book of Maccabees, again waged holy wars. Indeed, the external circumstances even approximated in a curious way the oldest forms of the holy war. No king commanded the army, nor was it organized by a state bureaucracy; it was not soldiers, but the mass of the rural Jewish population who fought for their faith and for the worship of the God of their fathers. Whether Judas is still to be understood as a charismatic in the old sense of the term is another question. If we test the conception of [war in] 1 Maccabees with that question in mind, a glaring deficiency becomes evident. It is true that the religious military speeches play a great role,[7] but that contrasts with the

---

6. Jer. 17:5-8 should be mentioned here, too, for the description of "trusting in Yahweh" and of the curse on false self-confidence is nothing other than a transposition of the old war motif to the level of the individual and the problems of human existence. It is the application to the individual of the call to faith which in Isaiah was still politically relevant to the people.

7. 1 Macc. 3:18-22, 58-60; 4:8-11; 5:32; 9:8, 44-46; 13:3-6.

strange secular conception of how the military events actually unfolded. "It is . . . remarkable that the successes with which the Maccabean enterprises were crowned are almost nowhere [in the texts] attributed to any immediate supernatural intervention on the part of God, but are represented throughout as the result of the military skill and political wisdom of the Maccabean princes."[8] Thus, when we read, as Elias J. Bickermann also emphasizes, that God neither wakens the hearts nor intervenes anywhere directly in the story, it certainly signifies a very radical shift.[9] It is hardly explained sufficiently with a reference to the significantly different literary technique of the historian—that is, to a more restrained, "indirect" portrayal. In the final analysis, this historian is still very much more concerned for the δοξασθῆναι of the Jews (1 Macc. 11:51) than for the portrayal of the astounding deeds of God in history. But Bickermann has taught us that the conceptions of the various historical relationships must be understood each from its own perspective. And that is why the question of whether the spirit of this historiography coincides with the spirit in which those wars were actually waged must remain open.

8. Emil Schürer, *A History of the Jewish People in the Time of Jesus Christ,* 2/III (New York: Scribner's, 1891): 7; *The Literature of the Jewish People in the Time of Jesus* (New York: Schocken, 1972), 7.

9. Elias J. Bickermann, *The God of the Maccabees: Studies on the Meaning and Origin of the Maccabean Revolt.* Studies in Judaism in Late Antiquity 32 (Leiden: Brill, 1979): 17.

War, Peace, and Justice in the Hebrew Bible: A Representative Bibliography

Judith E. Sanderson

THIS BIBLIOGRAPHY HAS BEEN PREPARED as a contribution to the advancement of peace in our world and in our communities. The need for it stems from the fact that the Bible seems to give conflicting messages about war and peace. If in Isa. 66:13 God promises to comfort Jerusalem as a mother comforts her child, the following three verses speak of God's anger and indignation, attacking enemies with fire, sword, and chariots like the whirlwind, and killing many. If Micah dreams of a golden future when nations will beat their swords into plowshares (Mic. 4:3; cf. Isa. 2:4), Joel calls the nations to beat their plowshares into swords (Joel 3:10). How do these passages fit together? What did they mean to the ancient Israelites? Which of them are relevant for Christians today, and how?

Christians who accept the Bible as in some sense authoritative for their imagining, their thinking, and their living need help to understand better what the Bible is all about and what its authority is. One of the greatest areas of trouble with the Hebrew Bible is its

1. I would like to thank Sandra Hughes Boyd and John Howard Yoder for reading the first draft and making very helpful suggestions. I am also grateful to Ben C. Ollenburger for providing annotations for several of the works included here.

militaristic flavor. God is presented as a mighty warrior who seems to love to slaughter the enemy. Is this the God whom Christians are called to emulate? Israel is portrayed as going to war against its neighbors again and again. Is this the example Christians are to follow? David killed and conquered and founded an empire. Is this "the man after God's own heart" (1 Sam. 13:14; Acts 13:22)?

As someone with a lifelong fascination for the Bible as well as a commitment to peacemaking, I must admit that these aspects of myself frequently seem in conflict with each other. Many of my students and friends have a similar ambivalence toward the Hebrew Bible. With the conviction that we who are called to work for peace with justice in our lives and in our world need help in understanding the Bible—first on its own terms, and then as a force in our lives—I have prepared this bibliography.

It is intended especially for Christian students, pastors, and teachers who want to read more themselves, as well as to recommend works to their parishioners and students, about the concepts and practice of war in the Hebrew Bible and about the relationship between war in the Bible and Christian views on war today. Also included is a selection of more technical resources to enable more detailed examination and study. An attempt has been made to represent the wide variety of perspectives among Christian denominations and movements struggling with issues of war and peace. Only those works other than and since Gerhard von Rad's are included. For von Rad's works and those of earlier scholars, see the introductory essay in this volume by Ben C. Ollenburger.

The rationale for the outline is as follows. After beginning with "General Works" broad enough to serve as introductions to the topic of war and peace in the Hebrew Bible, the focus narrows to the biblical "Imagery of Yahweh[2] as Divine Warrior and King." These two images belong inextricably together as central aspects

---

2. Many Jews consider the Hebrew name for God too sacred to be pronounced. Out of respect the name is often written without vowels to indicate its special nature.

of God in the Bible, they were taken together from the surrounding culture, they permeate the Bible, and they must be dealt with by Christians today as constituting a profoundly significant element of the biblical portrait of God. The next topic is the notion of "'Holy War' or 'Yahweh War' in the Hebrew Bible," a distinct but related theme which likewise appears throughout the Bible in a variety of forms and for a variety of purposes. There follow a few books by archaeologists and historians who deal with the military aspects of "The Conduct of Warfare in the Hebrew Bible." Since warfare involves political organization and power, and since one of the chief duties of the king was military defense, the next topic is "Political Power and Modes of Government in the Hebrew Bible." This section is subdivided: after "General Treatments" which provide overviews of the topic throughout the Hebrew Bible are listed others which focus on organization and government during "The Tribal Period" and finally during "The Monarchy." As is true of Yahweh theologically—the two images of warrior and king belong together—so it is with Israel's history: we must look at its wars and its kings together.

The focus then shifts to ideas of "Violence, Peace, and Justice in the Hebrew Bible." "Shalom" is not merely an antonym for war referring only to the absence of conflict; it is a positive and comprehensive term referring broadly to wholeness and well-being of community and individual. Thus it entails an equally broad sense of justice: legal, economic, racial, and sexual. Following a subsection of "General Works" are works which focus more specifically on issues of economic, sexual, racial, and worldwide justice. The final section, "Using the Bible for Nonviolent Ethics Today," includes works focusing on hermeneutical and ethical issues critical to Christians' understanding of the Bible in their efforts at peacemaking.

The categories divide the works for the reader's convenience only. The attempt has been made to classify each work according to its most significant contribution, but of course many works touch on more than one category. Sometimes this has been indicated by cross-reference.

Whenever applicable, the works within each category are divided according to audience. The "broad audience" would include specialists and nonspecialists alike; works in these sections can be recommended by teachers to students wishing a general introduction and, in the case of many, by pastors to parishioners with concern for these issues. "Technical works" generally use Hebrew and often other ancient Near Eastern languages (though often in transliteration) and/or presuppose a rather detailed knowledge of ancient history and cultures, or literary or sociological theory. When a section is not divided, it can be assumed that all the works listed are suitable for a wider audience.

The literature in this field is vast. The following are only representative titles in the various categories to suggest the wide range of topics which have been treated from a variety of perspectives. Preference has usually been given to works available in English and more recent works. These refer the reader to works in other languages and to earlier works, for those who wish to explore these issues more deeply. In general, if an author has written an entire book within this field, only that work is listed; citation to earlier articles by the same writer will be found in the listed book. Most of the listed works contain bibliographies citing further literature.

I. General Works
II. Imagery of Yahweh as Divine Warrior and King
    A. Works Suitable for a Broad Audience
    B. Technical Works
III. "Holy War" or "Yahweh War" in the Hebrew Bible
    A. Works Suitable for a Broad Audience
    B. Technical Works
IV. The Conduct of Warfare in the Hebrew Bible
V. Political Power and Modes of Government in the
    Hebrew Bible
    A. General Treatments
    B. The Tribal Period

I. General Works

These works cover a wide range of issues, including the imagery of Yahweh as warrior and king and the concepts of war and of government in the Hebrew Bible. All of these serve as introductions to the general field for specialists and nonspecialists alike.

Barrett, Lois. *The Way God Fights: War and Peace in the Old Testament.* Peace and Justice 1. Scottdale, Pa.: Herald, 1987. 79 pp. A Mennonite teaching minister provides a helpful introduction to a pacifist interpretation.

Craigie, Peter C. *The Problem of War in the Old Testament.* Grand Rapids: Wm. B. Eerdmans, 1978. 125 pp. One of the best places to start, providing an easily accessible general overview of the issues, written by a Hebrew Bible scholar but aimed at lay readers as well as Christian educators. Very sensitive treatment of "the problem of God, of revelation, and of ethics."

Eller, Vernard. *War and Peace from Genesis to Revelation: King*

Jesus' Manual of Arms for the 'Armless. Rev. ed. Scottdale, Pa.: Herald, 1981. 216 pp. Breezy introduction by a religion professor to a pacifist (Church of the Brethren) interpretation, arguing that the Bible's language of war is actually a message of peace.

Hanson, Paul D. "War and Peace in the Hebrew Bible." *Interp* 38 (1984): 341-362. An Old Testament professor traces the destinies of shalom (a sphere defined by worship, righteousness, and compassion) and its true opposite, chaos—not war!—throughout Israel's history. See also Hanson, "War, Peace and Justice in Early Israel." *Bible Review* 3 (1987): 32-45.

Janzen, Waldemar. "War in the Old Testament." *The Mennonite Quarterly Review* 46 (1972): 155-166. [Repr. in Janzen, *Still in the Image: Essays in Biblical Theology and Anthropology,* 173-186. Institute of Mennonite Studies Series 6. Newton, Kans.: Faith and Life and Winnipeg: CMBC, 1982.] A Mennonite Old Testament scholar considers "war as a topic in Old Testament theology, as a theological problem, and as a human reality, God as warrior, holy war, and the coming reign of peace."

Lind, Millard C. *Yahweh Is a Warrior: The Theology of Warfare in Ancient Israel.* Scottdale, Pa.: Herald, 1980. 232 pp. A Mennonite Old Testament specialist provides the technical exegetical basis for a pacifist interpretation of the Pentateuch and Deuteronomistic history. Argues that Yahweh's early position as sole warrior and sole king arose in the experience of the Exodus, "the fundamental paradigm for Israel's holy war . . . [and] 'prophetic' political structure." Only as Israel became like the nations (a process which began when they exchanged their prophetic leadership for a king) did Yahweh wage war against the people.

Tate, Marvin E. "War and Peacemaking in the Old Testament." *Review and Expositor* 79 (1982): 587-596. Southern Baptist Old Testament professor discusses five hermeneutical approaches to Old Testament war and relates the scholarly discussions to peacemaking today.

von Waldow, H. Eberhard. "The Concept of War in the Old Testament." *Horizons in Biblical Theology* 6 (1984): 27-48. An Old Testament theologian insists that the starting point of reflection is God as creator of a world of ordered diversity yet also of humankind as a unity (Gen. 1), which means that both division into nations (Gen. 10) and warfare represent sin. The sacredness of premonarchical war reflected belief in God's sovereign activity, while the formation of the state brought secularization as kings usurped God's prerogative.

Zimmerli, Walther. *The Old Testament and the World.* Atlanta: John Knox and London: SCM, 1976. "The People and Its Enemies," 53-66. A German Old Testament theologian surveys the topic of war within the Old Testament, emphasizing the notion of Israel's God-given right to live as God's people and to defend that right.

II. Imagery of Yahweh as Divine Warrior and King

These works focus primarily on two central and closely related aspects of the biblical portrait of God—the images of divine warrior and king—their antecedents in ancient Near Eastern mythologies, and their meaning for Christians today. Many writers find the imagery, especially that of warrior, troubling, as is evident from some of their titles. Their reflections, from varying perspectives, may enable readers to reach new insights into the meaning and use of biblical images for God.

A. *Works Suitable for a Broad Audience*

Bergant, Dianne. "Yahweh: A Warrior-God?" *TBT* 21 (1983): 156-161. A Roman Catholic Old Testament scholar explains what this imagery meant to Israel and urges Christians to find imagery more appropriate to the situation today.

Christ, Carol P. "Feminist Liberation Theology and Yahweh as Holy Warrior: An Analysis of Symbol." In *Women's Spirit Bonding,* ed. Janet Kalven and Mary I. Buckley, 202-212. New York: Pilgrim, 1984. A post-Christian feminist repudiates the imagery of a warrior God because of its profound symbolic influence on patriarchal and militaristic mindsets.

Coogan, Michael David, ed. *Stories from Ancient Canaan.* Philadelphia: Westminster, 1978. 120 pp. A very readable translation of Ugaritic myths with helpful introductions which highlight similarities with the Hebrew Bible. See especially the Introduction and the section on Baal.

Janzen, Waldemar. "God as Warrior and Lord: A Conversation with G. E. Wright." *BASOR* 220 (1975): 73-75. [Repr. in Janzen, *Still in the Image: Essays in Biblical Theology and Anthropology,* 187-192. Institute of Mennonite Studies Series 6. Newton, Kans.: Faith and Life and Winnipeg: CMBC, 1982.] A Mennonite Old Testament scholar responds to the work of his former professor, a Presbyterian (see below): the biblical order is not first Lord, symbolizing order, followed by Warrior, symbolizing restoration of order, but rather the reverse.

McCurley, Foster R. *Ancient Myths and Biblical Faith: Scriptural Transformations.* Philadelphia: Fortress, 1983. 192 pp. Traces in a lively way the successive uses of imagery of conflict, sexuality, and the sacred mountain, first in Mesopotamian, Canaanite, and Egyptian mythology, then in the Hebrew Bible, and finally in the New Testament. See especially Part I: "Order Versus Chaos: The Cyclical Conflict; Yahweh, Warrior and King; and The Son of God Versus Chaos" (11-71).

Mettinger, Tryggve N. D. *In Search of God: The Meaning and Message of the Everlasting Names.* Philadelphia: Fortress, 1988. 251 pp. A Swedish Old Testament scholar provides a very readable discussion, including helpful presentation of statistics, of two central designations which express complementary aspects of the royal metaphor: "The Lord as 'King': The Battling Deity" (ch. 6, 92-122: the pattern chaos battle—kingship—temple, displacing Baal) and " 'The Lord of Hosts': The Regnant God" (ch. 7, 123-157: enthroned on the cherubim and surrounded by the hosts of heaven, displacing El).

Miller, Patrick D., Jr. "God the Warrior: A Problem in Biblical Interpretation and Apologetics." *Interp* 19 (1965): 39-46. A Presbyterian Old Testament theologian argues that the imagery must be retained as an affirmation of God's activity and sovereignty in human history, evoking a response of trust without fear. (See II.B below for Miller's fuller treatment of this topic.)

Nysse, Richard. "Yahweh Is a Warrior." *Word and World* 7 (1987): 192-201. A Lutheran seminary professor insists that the warrior imagery be retained, because—but only insofar as—it calls the believer to petition and doxology, admitting dependence upon God.

Soggin, J. Alberto. "The Prophets on Holy War as Judgement against Israel." In *Old Testament and Oriental Studies,* 67-81. Biblica et Orientalia 29. Rome: Pontifical Biblical Institute, 1975. In their return to holy war ideology, the prophets do not view holy war as God acting against the nations through Israel; rather, they establish a "dialectical" relation in which the sword can be turned in the other direction—against Israel itself.

Tsevat, Matitiahu. "King, God as." *IDBS,* 515-16. Treats two origins and meanings of the idea: the mythical (king of the gods) and the societal (king of the people).

Wright, G. Ernest. *The Old Testament and Theology.* New York: Harper & Row, 1969). After ch. 4 on "God as Lord" (i.e., suzerain in relation to vassal Israel, an image similar to that of king), this Old Testament archaeologist and theologian then discusses in ch. 5 "God the Warrior" (121-150), surveying both the biblical imagery for God and its notion of war. He insists that theology must retain the image since, in a world which is a battleground, God the Warrior-Lord must be understood as the necessary counterpart of God the Lover-Redeemer.

B. Technical Works

Clifford, Richard J. *The Cosmic Mountain in Canaan and the Old Testament.* HSM 4. Cambridge, Mass.: Harvard University Press, 1972. 221 pp. Shows the relationships between El's mountain and Israel's Sinai traditions, and between Baal's Mt. Zaphon and Israel's Zion traditions.

Conrad, Edgar W. *Fear Not Warrior: A Study of* 'al tîrā' *Pericopes in the Hebrew Scriptures.* Brown Judaic Studies 75. Chico: Scholars Press, 1985. A form-critical study exploring the use of conventional language associated with the formula "Fear not!" throughout the Hebrew Bible. Finds two major uses: to order warriors to active participation in battle (in the Mosaic tradition) and to order kings, and the community as king, to passivity in war, allowing God to fight alone (in the Davidic tradition). Concludes that in Israel's imagination were two paradigmatic warriors: Joshua, actively involved in fighting; and Abraham, for whom Yahweh waged peace.

Cross, Frank Moore, Jr. *Canaanite Myth and Hebrew Epic: Essays in the History of the Religion of Israel.* Cambridge, Mass.: Harvard University Press, 1973. 376 pp. Argues from Israel's earliest poetry that the imagery of Yahweh as warrior and king was adopted very early from Canaanite mythology. See especially his treatments of "The Divine Warrior," "The Song of the Sea and Canaanite Myth," and "Yahweh and Ba'l" (91-194).

Day, John. *God's Conflict with the Dragon and the Sea: Echoes of a Canaanite Myth in the Old Testament.* University of Cambridge Oriental Studies 35. Cambridge: Cambridge University Press, 1985. 230 pp. Argues, *inter alia,* for the exclusively Canaanite origins of the imagery, for specifically Jebusite mediation of the Zion tradition via the cult of the god Elyon, and for at least a Solomonic date and the autumn festival of Yahweh's enthronement as the *Sitz im Leben* of Exod. 15:1-18.

Gray, John. *The Biblical Doctrine of the Reign of God.* Edinburgh: T. & T. Clark, 1979. 401 pp. Defends and develops, on the basis of Ugaritic influence, Sigmund Mowinckel's thesis of the antiquity and centrality of the Israelite notion of the kingship of Yahweh and of the autumn enthronement festival. Traces the motif throughout the Christian Bible.

Miller, Patrick D., Jr. *The Divine Warrior in Early Israel.* HSM 5. Cambridge, Mass.: Harvard University Press, 1973. 279 pp. Traces the imagery of divine warrior, divine assembly/council, and divine armies in Ugarit and throughout the Hebrew Bible.

Ollenburger, Ben C. *Zion, The City of the Great King: A Theological Symbol of the Jerusalem Cult.* JSOT Supplement 41. Sheffield: JSOT Press, 1987. 271 pp. Argues that Zion symbolized Yahweh's sole kingship and exclusive prerogative, and thus functioned positively to curb monarchical and military power and to promote justice. Concludes with theological and ethical implications for North American Christians today.

Schmid, H. H. "Heiliger Krieg und Gottesfrieden im alten Testament." In *Altorientalische Welt in der alttestamentlichen Theologie*, 91-120. Zurich: Theologischer Verlag, 1972. Conceptions of cosmic order (shalom), common to the ancient Near East, lie behind the Old Testament's theology of holy war. Yahweh's wars are to restore order that has been fractured.

Smith, Mark S. *The Early History of God: Yahweh and the Other Deities in Ancient Israel*. San Francisco: Harper & Row, 1990. 197 pp. One of the most recent and most comprehensive volumes on the subject of Yahweh's relationship to the Canaanite deities, drawing on recent discoveries and analyzing all the data. See especially ch. 1, "Deities in Israel in the Period of the Judges," and ch. 2, "Yahweh and Baal," with its excursus, "Yahweh and Anat."

Steck, Odil Hannes. *Friedensvorstellungen im alten Jerusalem: Psalmen, Jesaja, Deuterojesaja*. Theologische Studien 111. Zurich: Theologischer Verlag, 1972. 75 pp. Argues that Yahweh is the source of Jerusalem's peace as creator and sustainer from Zion, and world peace is achieved by the nations entering into the peace of Jerusalem. Foreign powers such as Assyria (in Isaiah) and Cyrus (in Deutero-Isaiah) can be used by Yahweh to restore peace.

Stolz, Fritz. *Jahwes und Israels Krieg: Kriegstheorien und Kriegserfahrungen im Glauben des alten Israel*. Abhandlungen zur Theologie des Alten und Neuen Testaments 60. Zurich: Theologischer Verlag, 1972. 211 pp. The Deuteronomistic theory of holy war is a theological and literary fiction. It draws from Israel's diverse experiences of warfare and unites this diversity within a theological framework provided by mythological traditions of divine warfare, at home in Jerusalem, and their modification in Deuteronomistic theology.

Stuart, Douglas. "The Sovereign's Day of Conquest." *BASOR* 221 (1976): 159-164. The ultimate origin of "the day of Yahweh" is found in thirteen ancient Near Eastern references to a notion of the sovereign's complete war of conquest being won in a single day.

III. "Holy War" or "Yahweh War" in the Hebrew Bible

Scholars debate whether there even is such a thing as "holy war" in the Bible, either as a concept or as a historical phenomenon, and if so, what it should be called and what its origins and nature were. Was there a uniform system of concepts and activities such that it could be called an institution? Was it an ancient concept and/or ancient practice, or did the idea first arise during the Monarchy? If ancient, was it the institution of a tribal confederation? (Martin Noth's idea of a specific type of confederation, an "amphictyony," is now largely discredited, and the nature of whatever cohesion existed is disputed.) Was it a cultic institution? Who provided leadership, and on what authority? These questions and others are debated in the works below.

A. Works Suitable for a Broad Audience

Good, Robert M. "The Just War in Ancient Israel." *JBL* 104 (1985): 385-400. Argues that Yahweh waged war primarily in the capacity of judge, which means that just war principles can be used "for a historically responsible moral critique of war in ancient Israel."

Gottwald, Norman K. "War, Holy." *IDBS*, 942-44. Updates Lawrence E. Toombs' article (see below), discussing more recent research and theories about the conduct and ideology of holy war throughout the Bible.

Jones, Gwilym H. " 'Holy War' or 'Yahweh War'?" *VT* 25 (1975): 642-658. In response to von Rad and Rudolf Smend, proposes that "Yahweh war" be used for the historical experience of Yahweh's participation in early war (which was neither amphictyonic nor cultic), while "holy war" be reserved for the later formulation/schematization.

Smend, Rudolf. *Yahweh War and Tribal Confederation: Reflections upon Israel's Earliest History.* Nashville: Abingdon, 1970. 144 pp. (Translated from the second German edition of 1966; the first appeared in 1963.) Responding to Noth and von Rad, rejects the term "holy war" and finds two distinct traditions in early Israel: Yahweh war (Exodus, Moses, political-military event, major judges, ark, Rachel tribes) in tension with tribal confederation (Sinai covenant, sacral-cultic institution, minor judges, central sanctuary, Leah tribes).

Toombs, Lawrence E. "War, Ideas of." *IDB*, 4:796-801. A concise and clearly organized overview of holy war, its concepts, history, prophetic and apocalyptic use, and its role in the New Testament. See also the article in *IDBS* by Norman K. Gottwald.

B. Technical Works

Craigie, Peter C. "Deborah and Anat: A Study of Poetic Imagery (Judges 5)." *ZAW* 90 (1978): 374-381. Argues that the poem dramatizes Deborah's role by evoking five images of Anat: her being assisted by a male warrior, and her roles as leader of warriors, as mistress of dominion, as maiden, and as mistress of the stars.

Cross, Frank Moore, Jr. *Canaanite Myth and Hebrew Epic: Essays in the History of the Religion of Israel.* Cambridge, Mass.: Harvard University Press, 1973. 376 pp. (See II.B above.)

DeVries, Simon J. "Temporal Terms as Structural Elements in the Holy-War Tradition." *VT* 25 (1975): 80-105. Studies the function of "today," "tomorrow," etc. in seven holy war narratives.

Fretz, Mark. "Herem in the Old Testament: A Critical Reading." In *Essays on War and Peace: Bible and Early Church*, ed. Willard M. Swartley, 7-44. Occasional Papers 9. Elkhart: Institute of Mennonite Studies, 1986. Finds great diversity in meaning and usage of this word ("destroy utterly"), ranging from "a nationalistic weapon [to] the tool for chastizing God's people."

Kang, Sa-Moon. *Divine War in the Old Testament and in the Ancient Near East.* BZAW 177. Berlin: de Gruyter, 1989. 251 pp. Attempts a comprehensive investigation of the motifs of divine war in the ancient Near East and of Yahweh war in Israel. Divine warfare began, in each case, with kingship, and there is nothing unique about divine war in the Old Testament texts.

Miller, Patrick D., Jr. *The Divine Warrior in Early Israel.* HSM 5.

Cambridge, Mass.: Harvard University Press, 1973. 279 pp. (See
II.B above.)

Rofé, Alexander. "The Laws of Warfare in the Book of Deuteronomy:
Their Origins, Intent and Positivity." *JSOT* 32 (1985): 23-44. An
Israeli biblical scholar doubts the existence of a uniform institution of "holy war" and argues in any case that these laws, so
often considered to refer to holy war, are far removed from
ancient war concepts and practices as seen elsewhere in the Bible.

Weimar, Peter. "Die Jahwekriegserzählungen in Exodus 14, Josua 10,
Richter 4 und 1 Samuel 7." *Bibl* 57 (1976): 38-73. Argues that
these four narratives of Yahweh war belong together as a group
that originated with conservative northerners in David's court as
a means of critique against the monarchy and its claims.

Weinfeld, Moshe. "Divine Intervention in War in Ancient Israel and in
the Ancient Near East." In *History, Historiography and Interpretation: Studies in Biblical and Cuneiform Literatures,* ed. Hayim
Tadmor and Weinfeld, 121-147. Jerusalem: Magnes, 1983. Argues
that stars fighting from heaven, fire and cloud, thunder and
lightning, hailstones, and prolonged daylight, rather than being
unique to Israel's portrayal of war, are paralleled in 2nd-millennium
Egyptian and Hittite war narratives and the Homeric epic.

Weippert, Manfred. " 'Heiliger Krieg' in Israel und Assyrien:
Kritische Anmerkungen zu Gerhard von Rads Konzept des 'Heiligen Krieges im alten Israel.' " *ZAW* 84 (1972): 460-493. On the
basis of Mari, Hittite, and Neo-Assyrian evidence of cultic activities in war and portrayal of divine intervention on their behalf,
Weippert rejects von Rad's view of Israel's war as a distinctive
and sacral institution; rather, Israel's practice and ideology of war
were common to the ancient world. It is correct to speak of
"Yahweh war" only in the same way one speaks of "Ishtar war."

IV. The Conduct of Warfare in the Hebrew Bible

These archaeological and historical works describe warfare in
ancient Israel: its personnel, organization, matériel, and methods.
All are accessible to a wide variety of readers.

Hobbs, T. R. *A Time for War: A Study of Warfare in the Old Testament.* Old Testament Studies 3. Wilmington: Michael Glazier, 1989. 248 pp. Hobbs' aim is to describe ancient Israelite warfare—the men, matériel, and art of war—and to discuss some related historical and literary issues, in order to provide a more accurate and realistic basis upon which Christians may go on to debate the theology of divine warrior and Israel's war.

De Vaux, Roland. *Ancient Israel.* 1: *Social Institutions.* New York: McGraw-Hill, 1965. 267 pp. A major work by a French biblical archaeologist describes life in Israel. See especially Part III (213-267): Military Institutions (The Armies of Israel, Fortified Cities and Siege Warfare, Armaments, War, The Holy War).

Wevers, John W. "War, Methods of." *IDB,* 4:801-5. Provides a concise overview of relevant issues, including the geography of Palestine, military routes, fortresses, and siege warfare. Also, "Weapons and Implements of War." *IDB,* 4:820-25. Traces the development of weapons from the Stone Age until the Iron Age, with a careful description of individual offensive (e.g., spear, javelin) and defensive (shield, armor) weapons.

Yadin, Yigael. *The Art of Warfare in Biblical Lands in the Light of Archaeological Study.* Jerusalem: International and New York: McGraw-Hill, 1963. 2 vols., 484 pp. Written by one of Israel's leading archaeologists and profusely illustrated in black and white and color.

V. Political Power and Modes of Government in the Hebrew Bible

A. General Treatments

These works, all usable by a wide audience, discuss power and political organization throughout the Hebrew Bible, thus serving as helpful introductions to this topic, which is critical because of its relationship to the topic of war.

Mendenhall, George E. "Government, Israelite." *IDBS,* 372-75. A very good, brief introduction to Mendenhall's theories of the emergence of Israel and of the monarchy, beginning with a description of Bronze Age governments and concluding with "the New Testament reformation." (See also his articles regarding the tribal period and the Monarchy, below.)

De Vaux, Roland. *Ancient Israel.* 1: *Social Institutions.* New York: McGraw-Hill, 1965. 267 pp. Provides archaeological and historical understanding of life in Israel. See especially Part II (65-177), with its extensive treatment of civil institutions, including: The Israelite Concept of the State, The Person of the King, The Royal Household, The Principal Officials of the King, The Administration of the Kingdom, Finance and Public Works, Law and Justice, and Economic Life.

Walsh, J. P. M. *The Mighty from Their Thrones: Power in the Biblical Tradition.* OBT 21. Philadelphia: Fortress, 1987. 206 pp. A Jesuit Old Testament specialist who subscribes to the peasant revolt theory (see below, "The Tribal Period") distinguishes the early Israelite and the Canaanite views of justice and power and traces the destinies of these systems through the Christian Bible, drawing along the way implications for a theology and ethics of liberation.

B. The Tribal Period

Three basic models currently are being debated for understanding the origins of Israel: conquest (William F. Albright, G. Ernest Wright, and Paul W. Lapp), peaceful infiltration (Albrecht Alt, Martin Noth, and Manfred Weippert), and, most recently, peasant revolt (George E. Mendenhall and Norman K. Gottwald). Our understanding of the way in which Israel emerged will have a major impact on our interpretation of the portrayal of its early warfare — its occurrence, its motivations, its nature, and its extent — as well as of the portrayal of military, political, and religious leadership, and also the lives of ordinary people during the early centuries of Israel's existence. These models and related issues of power and leadership are discussed in the works below.

1. Works Suitable for a Broad Audience

Anderson, Bernhard W. "Mendenhall Disavows Paternity: Says He Didn't Father Gottwald's Marxist Theory." *Bible Review* 2/2 (1986): 46-49. A very accessible overview of all three models as well as the disagreement between Mendenhall and Gottwald.

Brueggemann, Walter. *Revelation and Violence: A Study in Contextualization.* Milwaukee: Marquette University Press, 1986. 72 pp. A highly readable study of Josh. 11 following Gottwald, combining methods of sociological and literary analysis, and addressing the question: "How are these texts of violence to be understood as revelation" both to the ancient Israelites and to Christians today?

Hackett, Jo Ann. "Women's Studies and the Hebrew Bible." In *The Future of Biblical Studies: The Hebrew Scriptures,* ed. Richard E. Friedman and H. G. M. Williamson, 141-164. SBL Semeia Studies. Atlanta: Scholars Press, 1987. A Hebrew Bible scholar discusses methods and questions of the new women's history (e.g., the positive effect of social disruption on women's participation contrasted with the negative effect of centralization on their participation), illustrating their use in her study of the lives and sources of power of women—and, by extension, of all people—in Judg. 3–16.

Meyers, Carol L. *Discovering Eve: Ancient Israelite Women in Context.* New York: Oxford University Press, 1988. 238 pp. An archaeologist applies social-scientific methods and the peasant revolt model to the question of the status of women during the tribal period, providing a very illuminating view of daily life, from cisterns to terracing to house and family size, and offers her distinctive interpretation of Gen. 2–3.

2. Technical Works

Ackerman, James S. "Prophecy and Warfare in Early Israel: A Study of the Deborah-Barak Story." *BASOR* 220 (1975): 5-13. Argues for premonarchical origin of prophecy, since this narrative shows Deborah as prophet commissioning Barak as war leader and proclaiming assurance of victory.

Biblical Archaeology Today. Jerusalem: Israel Exploration Society, 1985. Proceedings of the International Congress on Biblical Archaeology, Jerusalem, April 1984. David Noel Freedman, Norman K. Gottwald, Siegfried Herrmann, Moshe Kochavi, and Amihai Mazar, followed by five respondents, discuss the issue of the settlement in Canaan as a case study of the interactions of archaeological, historical, and biblical studies.

Freedman, David Noel, and Graf, David Frank, eds. *Palestine in Transition: The Emergence of Ancient Israel.* The Social World of Biblical Antiquity 2. Sheffield: Almond, 1983. 108 pp. William H. Stiebing, John M. Halligan, Norman K. Gottwald, Marvin L. Chaney, and George E. Mendenhall discuss political, social, economic, and archaeological issues involved in Mendenhall, "The Hebrew Conquest of Palestine" (see below), and Gottwald, *The Tribes of Yahweh* (see below), revealing the significant differences between the two approaches. Chaney's article introduces and evaluates all three models with extensive bibliography, proposing his own variation on the third: peasant and frontier revolt.

Fritz, Volkmar. "Conquest or Settlement? The Early Iron Age in Palestine." *BA* 50 (1987): 84-100. A German archaeologist analyzes recent archaeological findings, proposes a modification of the infiltration model, "the symbiosis hypothesis," and finds it supported by the Merneptah stele and Judg. 1 and 5.

Gottwald, Norman K. *The Tribes of Yahweh: A Sociology of the Religion of Liberated Israel, 1250–1050 B.C.E.* Maryknoll, N.Y.: Orbis, 1979. 916 pp. This monumental work employs methods of the social sciences as well as of biblical studies to argue that Israel emerged as an egalitarian movement in socio-economic and religio-political revolt against the economically oppressive, monarchical Canaanite city-states and in subsequent deliberate "retribalization."

Mendenhall, George E. "The Hebrew Conquest of Palestine." *BA* 25 (1962): 66-87. [Repr. with slight revisions in *The Biblical Archaeologist Reader* 3, ed. Edward F. Campbell, Jr., and David Noel Freedman, 100-120. Garden City: Doubleday, 1970.] The first suggestion of a new model of understanding Israel's emergence: as a peasant revolt against Canaanite city-states and creation of a tribal confederacy united in covenant with Yahweh.

C. The Monarchy

The Israelite monarchy emerged in a situation of severe controversy, which is mirrored today in scholarly debates about the historical, sociological, literary, and theological issues involved. Did the change from a tribal system to a monarchy represent a betrayal of what Israel was all about, a giving up of egalitarian ideals, and the beginning of exploitation? Or was it a natural step toward more sophisticated organization necessitated by the Philistine threat, and representing positive development economically, politically, and socially? How did the first kings legitimate their accession and their subsequent rule? Once the monarchy was in place, what were the attitudes of various groups toward the king, and what checks and balances to his power existed? How did the biblical texts about the change to monarchy arise, and how are they to be interpreted? The following works address these and related issues from a variety of perspectives and using a variety of critical methods.

1. Works Suitable for a Broad Audience

Brueggemann, Walter. *David's Truth in Israel's Imagination and Memory.* Philadelphia: Fortress, 1985. 128 pp. Describes four conflicting but "mutually corrective" views of David in the Deuteronomistic history, Pss. 89 and 132, and the Chronicler: "the trustful truth of the tribe, the painful truth of the man, the sure truth of the state, and the hopeful truth of the assembly."

Dulin, Rachel. "Anti-Davidic Voices." *TBT* 26 (1988): 267-271. A Jewish theologian discusses briefly the various kinds of criticism of David recorded in the Bible, reflecting on the freedom the writers felt to express political dissent.

Halpern, Baruch. "The Uneasy Compromise: Israel between League and Monarchy." In *Traditions in Transformation: Turning Points in Biblical Faith,* ed. Halpern and Jon D. Levenson, 59-96. Festschrift Frank M. Cross. Winona Lake: Eisenbrauns, 1981. Arguing that Israel's distinctive form of limited monarchy (as seen in its constitution, Deut. 17:14-20) represented a compromise between the tribes and the Shiloh priesthood, each of which retained much of its power, Halpern traces the power struggles of the periods of league and united kingdom.

Hoppe, Leslie J. "Deuteronomy on Political Power." *TBT* 26 (1988): 261-66. A Roman Catholic Old Testament specialist discusses briefly the vision of Deut. 16:18–18:22 for the rule of law, distribution of power, and limitations on the prerogatives of the king, all in the service of justice for every Israelite.

McCarthy, Dennis J. "The Inauguration of Monarchy in Israel: A Form-Critical Study of I Samuel 8–12." *Interp* 27 (1973): 401-412. Argues that the intention of the pericope was to describe in narrative and theological terms the fundamental crisis posed by monarchy as well as its resolution: the integration of kingship into Israel's covenant relationship with Yahweh.

Mendenhall, George E. "The Monarchy." *Interp* 29 (1975): 155-170. Emphasizing the interplay of social organization and ideology, a forceful repudiation of the monarchy as causing a total break from the Yahwist revolution and "a systematic reversion to Bronze Age paganism" within the first two generations.

Roberts, J. J. M. "In Defense of the Monarchy: The Contribution of Israelite Kingship to Biblical Theology." In *Ancient Israelite Religion: Essays in Honor of Frank Moore Cross,* ed. Patrick D. Miller, Jr., Paul D. Hanson, and S. Dean McBride, 377-396. Philadelphia: Fortress, 1987. Rejects the force of three current criticisms of the monarchy: its borrowing of significant elements from surrounding cultures, an alleged conflict between human and divine kingship, and the human motivations involved.

———. "Zion in the Theology of the Davidic-Solomonic Empire." In *Studies in the Period of David and Solomon,* ed. Tomoo Ishida, 93-108. Winona Lake: Eisenbrauns and Tokyo: Yamakawa-Shuppansha, 1982. Describes the main features of the Zion tradition, showing Canaanite antecedents, and argues for a "crystallization point" during David's reign. See also Roberts, "Zion Tradition," *IDBS,* 985-87.

Sziksai, Stephen. "King, Kingship." *IDB,* 3:11-17. Provides an overview of such topics as the emergence of kingship in Israel; the king's duties, cultic functions, officials, and revenue; divine kingship in the ancient Near East and in Israel; and the New Year festival.

2. Technical Works

Bernhardt, Karl-Heinz. *Das Problem der altorientalischen Königsideologie im alten Testament.* VTS 8. Leiden: Brill, 1961. 351 pp. A critical survey of scholarship on the Psalms against the background of Near Eastern royal ideologies. On this basis, Bernhardt denies the existence, in ancient Israel, of a royal ideology that ascribed sacral status to the king.

Birch, Bruce C. *The Rise of the Israelite Monarchy: The Growth and Development of 1 Samuel 7–15.* SBL Dissertation 27. Missoula: Scholars Press, 1976. 170 pp. Concludes that a number of old traditions with a generally positive attitude toward Saul circulated independently until the late 8th cent., when they were brought together along with new compositions into a single edition in northern prophetic circles. This prophetic edition portrayed Saul in a special relationship with God, anointed and endowed with God's spirit, hence especially responsible to obey God's law. The Deuteronomistic historian, in basic sympathy with that edition, incorporated it into his own work with only a few additions designed to make the view of kingship less positive.

Boecker, Hans-Jochen. *Die Beurteiling der Anfänge des Königtums in den deuteronomistischen Abschnitten des I. Samuelbuches.* WMANT 31. Neukirchen-Vluyn: Neukirchener, 1969. 99 pp. Passages in 1 Samuel previously interpreted as rejecting kingship are viewed instead as offering merely a critique. The Deuteronomists drew on Deut. 17, which subjects royal behavior to divine law, to show the tension between the stability kingship provides and the burden it imposes.

Clements, Ronald E. "The Deuteronomistic Interpretation of the Founding of the Monarchy in I Sam. VIII." *VT* 24 (1974): 398-410. After seeking to reconcile the extremely unfavorable list of the ways of the king (1 Sam. 8:11-17) with Yahweh's subsequent allowance of a king, Clements concludes that, while the narrative is complex, the Deuteronomists' attitude toward the monarchy is simple: Davidic kings were acceptable to Yahweh because divinely chosen; other kings were not.

Cross, Frank Moore, Jr. *Canaanite Myth and Hebrew Epic: Essays in the History of the Religion of Israel.* Cambridge, Mass.: Harvard University Press, 1973. 376 pp. See especially ch. 9, "The Ideologies of Kingship in the Era of the Empire" (219-273), which traces the destinies of two royal ideologies: the conditional covenant of Saul and David surviving as an ideal in the northern kingdom, and the unconditional theology of divine sonship in Judah.

Crüsemann, Frank. *Der Widerstand gegen das Königtum: Die anti-königlichen Texte des alten Testaments und der Kampf um den frühen israelitischen Staat.* WMANT 49. Neukirchen-Vluyn: Neukirchener, 1978. 257 pp. Draws on anthropological parallels to suggest that opposition to monarchy, as expressed in Judges and 1 Samuel, stemmed from premonarchic Israel's status as a segmentary lineage system in which political power is distributed through groups with equal status.

Eaton, John H. *Kingship and the Psalms.* SBT, 2nd ser. 32. Naperville: Alec R. Allenson and London: SCM, 1976. 227 pp. Identifies far more psalms as composed for the Davidic kings than did Hermann Gunkel, argues for their use in rites of renewal of the king's office at the autumn festival, and analyzes twenty-seven aspects of the ideal king as portrayed in these psalms (e.g., "the laws of the kingdom are God's," "the king's life benefits the people").

Eslinger, Lyle. "Viewpoints and Point of View in 1 Samuel 8–12." *JSOT* 26 (1983): 61-76. Applying narrative theory to this pericope, Eslinger finds its meaning in the guidance of "the omniscient narrator."

Frick, Frank S. *The Formation of the State in Ancient Israel: A Survey of Models and Theories.* The Social World of Biblical Antiquity 4. Sheffield: Almond, 1985. 219 pp. Presents models and data from archaeology, comparative ethnography, and biblical narratives to help biblical scholars understand the socio-political processes (especially those relating to agricultural intensification) on the path of "adaptive modification" from segmentary society ("tribal" period) to chiefdom (Saul) to state (David in Jerusalem).

Halpern, Baruch. *The Constitution of the Monarchy in Israel.* HSM 25. Chico: Scholars Press, 1981. 410 pp. The conditional royal covenant need not be relegated to the time of the Exile. The "assembly" and other tribal institutions were political entities existing in parallel with kingship during the monarchical period.

Ishida, Tomoo. *The Royal Dynasties in Ancient Israel: A Study on the Foundation and Development of Royal-Dynastic Ideology.* BZAW 142. Berlin: de Gruyter, 1976. 211 pp. The Israelite monarchy was unique in the ancient Near East because it arose due to political pressures and in the face of resistance. Anti-kingship arguments reflected in the Old Testament were not later editorial responses; instead, they were silenced by the time of David and Solomon. Davidic royal ideology was directed principally toward northern tribal acceptance of David's rule.

Mayes, A. D. H. "The Rise of the Israelite Monarchy." *ZAW* 90 (1978): 1-19. Accepts, with some modifications, Martin Noth's view that the Deuteronomist created 1 Sam. 8–12 by very skillfully combining a number of independent traditions with his own compositions. But the Deuteronomist's attitude toward the monarchy was ambivalent: realizing both the benefits (especially for justice) and the dangers, he showed the solution in 1 Sam. 12: submission to Yahweh's law.

Mettinger, Tryggve N. D. *King and Messiah: The Civil and Sacral Legitimation of the Israelite Kings.* Coniectanea Biblica, Old Testament 8. Lund: Gleerup, 1976. 342 pp. With special attention to the historical development of the conceptions involved and to the interdependence of civil and sacral aspects, a study of legitimation by civil (elders, assembly, acclamation, royal covenant) and sacral (divine designation, anointing, charisma, divine sonship, and Davidic covenant) means of the early kings.

Ollenburger, Ben C. *Zion, The City of the Great King: A Theological Symbol of the Jerusalem Cult.* JSOT Supplement 41. Sheffield: JSOT Press, 1987. 271 pp. (See II.B above.)

Seow, C. L. *Myth, Drama, and the Politics of David's Dance.* HSM 44. Atlanta: Scholars Press, 1989. 272 pp. Argues that Yahweh had already been identified with El at Shiloh, then with Baal at Kiriath-jearim, and that David's procession with the ark into

Jerusalem was a religio-political drama celebrating Yahweh's victory as divine warrior and accession as king, demonstrating David's authority as king, and inaugurating Jerusalem as capital.

Veijola, Timo. *Das Königtum in der Beurteilung der deuteronomistischen Historiographie: Eine redaktionsgeschichtliche Untersuchung.* Annales academiae scientiarum Fennicae, B, 108. Helsinki: Suomalainen Tiedcakatemia, 1977. 147 pp. Seeks to distinguish, through redaction-critical study, an earlier reflective and positive view of monarchy, as well as later reinterpretation and negative assessment. There are two Deuteronomists—one who finds kingship to be legitimate but is critical of bad kings, and another who condemns kingship itself as disobedient and entailing the people's rejection of Yahweh.

Weimar, Peter. "Die Jahwekriegserzählungen in Exodus 14, Josua 10, Richter 4 und 1 Samuel 7." *Bibl* 57 (1976): 38-73. (See III.B above.)

Whitelam, Keith W. *The Just King: Monarchical Judicial Authority in Ancient Israel.* JSOT Supplement 12. Sheffield: JSOT Press, 1979. 320 pp. Sample conclusions: royal practice diverged widely from the ideal portrayal of king as judge; whereas David was portrayed as the warrior *par excellence,* Solomon, in a major ideological development, was portrayed as the Just King *par excellence,* endowed with divine wisdom in judicial matters; the climax in the development was Jehoshaphat's reform, subordinating local and priestly judicial authority to the king's.

VI. Violence, Peace, and Justice in the Hebrew Bible

A. General Works

The following works deal with broad-ranging issues of peace with justice, both as they are addressed directly by the biblical text and as they face Christian interpreters today, who bring questions to the Bible from their own experience—including issues not necessarily recognized by the biblical writers themselves. Unless otherwise noted, they are suitable for a wide audience.

Birch, Bruce C. *What Does the Lord Require? The Old Testament Call to Social Witness.* Philadelphia: Westminster, 1985. 119 pp. Highly readable treatment by an Old Testament professor of "the particular elements of the Old Testament tradition that inform the church's contemporary social witness," including creation (which, symbolizing sustaining, blessing, and shalom, should be given priority over deliverance, symbolizing crisis intervention), exodus, and covenant.

Brueggemann, Walter. *Living Toward a Vision: Biblical Reflections on Shalom.* 2nd ed. New York: United Church Press, 1982. 201 pp. An Old Testament theologian discusses "a vision of shalom, freedom, and order, the shalom church, and shalom persons" in both testaments. Appendix provides "a shalom lectionary," with explanation, for each season of the church year.

————. *The Prophetic Imagination.* Philadelphia: Fortress, 1978. 127 pp. A stimulating work contrasting the "alternative community of Moses" with the "royal consciousness" and showing the prophetic responses of criticizing/pathos of Jeremiah, the energizing/amazement of Second Isaiah, and the combination of these in Jesus.

Donahue, John R. "Biblical Perspectives on Justice." In *The Faith That Does Justice: Examining the Christian Sources for Social Change,* ed. John C. Haughey, 68-112. New York: Paulist, 1977. A Jesuit New Testament specialist explores justice throughout the biblical literature and describes the Christian task today as translating the love of God into the doing of justice. A sample conclusion from the Old Testament: "The marginal groups in society . . . become the scale on which the justice of the whole society is weighed."

Gonzalez, Justo L., and Gonzalez, Catherine G. *Liberation Preaching: The Pulpit and the Oppressed.* Nashville: Abingdon, 1980. 127 pp. Highly illuminating and practical analysis of "difficulties in hearing the text" with insightful suggestions: e.g., "Ask the political question, reassign the case of characters, consider the direction of the action."

Gottwald, Norman K. *The Hebrew Bible: A Socio-Literary Introduction.* Philadelphia: Fortress, 1985. 702 pp. A scholarly introduction to biblical study and to each book of the Bible, based on traditional methods plus more recent critical, literary, and social-scientific approaches.

————, ed. *The Bible and Liberation: Political and Social Hermeneutics.* Maryknoll, N.Y.: Orbis, 1983. Twenty-eight articles, some rather technical, including: Sergio Rostagno, "The Bible: Is an Interclass Reading Legitimate?" (61-73); Carlos Mesters, "The Use of the Bible in Christian Communities of the Common People" (119-133); Kuno Füssel, "The Materialist Reading of the Bible" (134-146); Phyllis A. Bird, "Images of Women in the Old Testament" (252-288); Arthur F. McGovern, "The Bible in Latin American Liberation Theology" (461-472).

Klassen, William. *Love of Enemies: The Way to Peace.* OBT 15. Philadelphia: Fortress, 1984. 145 pp. A Mennonite New Testament scholar devotes one chapter to the theme of love of enemies in the Hebrew Bible and one to Second Temple writings.

Lohfink, Norbert, ed. *Gewalt und Gewaltlosigkeit im alten Testament.* Quaestiones Disputatae 96. Freiberg: Herder, 1983. 256 pp. Five essays by Roman Catholic Old Testament scholars and a systematic theologian, all sparked by René Girard's theory of violence (see Robert G. North, below).

Mott, Stephen Charles. *Biblical Ethics and Social Change.* New York: Oxford University Press, 1982. 254 pp. Treatment of the Hebrew Bible by this evangelical Methodist social ethicist is to be found especially in Part I, "A Biblical Theology of Social Involvement": ch. 4 (59-81), "God's Justice and Ours" (urging creative justice in the commitment to the oppressed); and ch. 5 (82-106),"The Long March of God" (God's reign brings an imperative for justice).

North, Robert G. "Violence and the Bible: The Girard Connection." *CBQ* 47 (1985): 1-27. A Jesuit biblical scholar tests René Girard's *Violence and the Sacred* (Baltimore: Johns Hopkins University Press, 1977) against the Bible.

Schwager, Raymund. *Must There Be Scapegoats? Violence and Redemption in the Bible.* San Francisco: Harper & Row, 1987. 243 pp. A Swiss Jesuit systematic theologian applies René Girard's theory in *Violence and the Sacred* to the Bible.

Topel, L. John. *The Way to Peace: Liberation Through the Bible.* Maryknoll, N.Y.: Orbis, 1979. 199 pp. A Jesuit theologian provides an easily accessible introduction both to the Bible and to liberation theology, with the theme: "the Bible reveals God and humankind cooperating in bringing a reign of justice and peace in our world."

Waish, J. P. M. *The Mighty from Their Thrones: Power in the Biblical Tradition.* OBT 21. Philadelphia: Fortress, 1987. 206 pp. (See V.A above.)

Yoder, Perry B. *Shalom: The Bible's Word for Salvation, Justice, and Peace.* Newton, Kans.: Faith and Life, 1987. 154 pp. A Mennonite Old Testament scholar (who rewrote the first draft of this book after four months in base Christian communities in the Philippines) explores the biblical descriptions of peace and its connections to other biblical themes, with the goal of awakening readers to a common vision of peace.

B. Works Focusing on Issues of Peace with Economic Justice

Gnuse, Robert. *You Shall Not Steal: Community and Property in the Biblical Tradition.* Maryknoll, N.Y.: Orbis, 1985. 162 pp. A Lutheran Old Testament specialist argues that the Seventh Commandment, far from legitimating the accumulation of excessive wealth, actually was interpreted by biblical traditions, legal and sermonic, to protect the poor and guarantee to all the basic necessities of life; he concludes with contemporary implications.

Haan, Roelf. *The Economics of Honour: Biblical Reflections on Money and Property.* Geneva: WCC, 1988. 71 pp. Fourteen brief meditations from a Dutch perspective on biblical passages, dealing with issues such as economic injustice, distribution, and the power of money.

Mason, John D. "Biblical Teaching and Assisting the Poor." *Trans-*

formation 4/2 (1987): 1-14. An evangelical economics professor describes the Pentateuch's "reasonably sophisticated set of assistance programmes characterized by 'compassionate stewardship' " and draws contemporary implications.

Mays, James Luther. "Justice: Perspectives from the Prophetic Tradition." *Interp* 37 (1983): 5-17. An Old Testament specialist who has written several commentaries on the prophets describes the social context of 8th-cent. Judah and the meaning of justice for Amos, Isaiah, and Micah.

Ringe, Sharon H. *Jesus, Liberation, and the Biblical Jubilee: Images for Ethics and Christology.* OBT 17. Philadelphia: Fortress, 1985. 124 pp. A New Testament specialist devotes ch. 2 (16-32) to "Jubilee Traditions in Hebrew Scriptures: A Cluster of Images," concluding that they always join God's sovereignty with a demand for justice in economic and social structures.

Sider, Ronald. "Toward a Biblical Perspective on Equality: Steps on the Way Toward Christian Political Engagement." *Interp* 43 (1989): 156-169. A Baptist seminary professor of theology and culture explores one aspect of a biblical paradigm on economic justice.

C. Works Focusing on Issues of Peace with Sexual Justice

Hackett, Jo Ann. "Women's Studies and the Hebrew Bible." In *The Future of Biblical Studies: The Hebrew Scriptures,* ed. Richard E. Friedman and H. G. M. Williamson, 141-164. SBL Semeia Studies. Atlanta: Scholars Press, 1987. (See V.B.1 above.)

Meyers, Carol. *Discovering Eve: Ancient Israelite Women in Context.* New York: Oxford University Press, 1988. 238 pp. (See V.B.1 above.)

Russell, Letty M., ed. *Feminist Interpretation of the Bible.* Philadelphia: Westminster, 1985. 166 pp. Probably the best one-volume introduction to feminist hermeneutics, with essays in theory and practice by specialists in theology, ethics, and biblical studies (ten white Roman Catholics and Protestants, one African-American, and one Jew).

Sakenfeld, Katharine Doob. "Feminist Biblical Interpretation." *Theology Today* 46 (1989): 154-168. Illustrates three methods of feminist interpretation with the example of Num. 27 and 36 (the daughters of Zelophehad) and analyzes their relative merits.

Trible, Phyllis. *God and the Rhetoric of Sexuality.* OBT 2. Philadelphia: Fortress, 1978. 206 pp. Uses rhetorical criticism to find positive images of God and women in Gen. 1–3, Ruth, Song of Songs, prophetic texts, etc.

D. Works Showing North Americans How the Bible Is Read around the World

Brown, Robert McAfee. *Unexpected News: Reading the Bible with Third World Eyes.* Philadelphia: Westminster, 1984. 166 pp. A North American theologian interprets "Third World" readings of biblical texts, including the stories of the Exodus, David and Nathan, and Jeremiah and Jehoiakim, to North Americans; accessible to all readers.

Fabella, Virginia, and Oduyoye, Mercy Amba, eds. *With Passion and Compassion: Third World Women Doing Theology.* Maryknoll, N.Y.: Orbis, 1988. 192 pp. Reflections from the Women's Commission of the Ecumenical Association of Third World Theologians. See especially Teresa Okure, from Nigeria, who finds both liberative and oppressive elements in the portrayal of "Women in the Bible" (47-59) and suggests new hermeneutical and pastoral principles; and Elsa Tamez, from Mexico, who discusses "Women's Rereading of the Bible" (173-180) and provides three guidelines for a Latin American women's perspective in rereading.

Fabella, Virginia, and Park, Sun Ai Lee, eds. *We Dare to Dream: Doing Theology as Asian Women.* Maryknoll, N.Y.: Orbis, 1990. 156 pp. See especially Lee Oo Chung, from Korea, who gives a Bible study on "Peace, Unification and Women"; and Elizabeth Dominguez, from the Philippines, who discusses creation, poverty, and prostitution in the "Biblical Concept of Human Sexuality: Challenge to Tourism."

Pobee, John S., and von Wartenberg-Potter, Bärbel, eds. *New Eyes for Reading: Biblical and Theological Reflections by Women from the Third World.* Geneva: WCC and Oak Park, Ill.: Meyer-Stone, 1986. 108 pp. Very illuminating, brief, and readable examples of how women around the world read biblical passages.

Tamez, Elsa. *Bible of the Oppressed.* Maryknoll, N.Y.: Orbis, 1982. 80 pp. A Latin American biblical scholar studies the biblical themes of oppression and liberation; careful exegesis accessible to all readers.

E. Works Focusing on Issues of the Interactions of Race, Class, and/or Sex

Cannon, Katie Geneva, and Schüssler Fiorenza, Elisabeth, eds. *Interpretation for Liberation.* Semeia 47 (1989). 153 pp. One Chinese and six African-American scholars propose and illustrate new approaches for a biblical hermeneutics of liberation.

Felder, Cain Hope. *Troubling Biblical Waters: Race, Class, and Family.* Maryknoll, N.Y.: Orbis, 1989. 233 pp. An African-American New Testament scholar deals with these three issues in both testaments.

Mosala, Itumeleng J. *Biblical Hermeneutics and Black Theology in South Africa.* Grand Rapids: Wm. B. Eerdmans, 1989. 218 pp. A Black South African biblical scholar argues for a materialist reading of the Bible, offering one for Micah and for Luke 1–2. While the theoretical sections are somewhat technical, the studies of Micah and Luke are accessible and can be read on their own.

Weems, Renita J. *Just a Sister Away: A Womanist Vision of Women's Relationships in the Bible.* San Diego: LuraMedia, 1988. 145 pp. Insightful, highly readable treatments of Hagar and Sarah, Naomi and Ruth, Miriam and her Cushite sister-in-law, etc., by an African-American Hebrew Bible scholar. Recommended for all readers.

VII. Using the Bible for Nonviolent Ethics Today

These works, suitable for a general audience, deal with hermeneutical and ethical issues involved in Christians' understanding and appropriation of the Bible in their efforts at peacemaking.

Aukerman, Dale. *Darkening Valley: A Biblical Perspective on Nuclear War.* New York: Seabury, 1981. 228 pp. An American involved in international peace work reflects on biblical passages and modern circumstances.

Enz, Jacob J. *The Christian and Warfare: The Roots of Pacifism in the Old Testament.* Scottdale, Pa.: Herald, 1972. A Mennonite argues that the roots (i.e., the covenant mode of relationship, limitations on absolute kingship, and reliance on God rather than on military supremacy) reveal implicit theological pacifism in preparation for explicit pacifism in the New Testament.

Janzen, Waldemar. "Christian Perspectives on War and Peace in the Old Testament." Council of Mennonite Studies *Occasional Papers* 1 (1981): 3-18. [Repr. in Janzen, *Still in the Image: Essays in Biblical Theology and Anthropology,* 193-211. Institute of Mennonite Studies Series 6. Newton, Kans.: Faith and Life and Winnipeg: CMBC, 1982.] A Mennonite scholar outlines three Christian approaches to warfare in the Hebrew Bible (God's victorious rule, preparation for God's coming rule, or failure of one form of God's rule), opting for the second.

Pawlikowski, John T., and Senior, Donald, eds. *Biblical and Theological Reflections on* The Challenge of Peace. Theology and Life 10. Wilmington: Michael Glazier, 1984. Roman Catholic theologians respond to the U.S. bishops' pastoral letter on war and peace. See especially these popular articles by Old Testament specialists: Dianne Bergant, in "Peace in a Universe of Order" (17-30), discusses two biblical themes: Yahweh as warrior and harmony in all of nature; Carroll Stuhlmueller, in "The Prophetic Prize for Peace" (31-44), describes four moments in the history of prophecy leading toward a vision of universal peace; and Leslie J. Hoppe, in "Religion and Politics" (45-54), provides "Paradigms from Early Judaism," including 1 and 2 Maccabees and Daniel.

Schmidt, Daryl. "The Biblical Hermeneutics on Peacemaking in the Bishops' Pastoral." *BTB* 16 (1986): 47-55. More technical than the chapters in Pawlikowski-Senior, this article analyzes and criticizes the bishops' assumptions in their use of the biblical texts.

Swaim, J. Carter. *War, Peace, and th Bible.* Maryknoll, N.Y.: Orbis, 1982. A Presbyterian New Testament specialist gives a very readable and compelling treatment of biblical themes and contemporary issues, replete with anecdotes and practical application.

Swartley, Willard M. *Slavery, Sabbath, War, and Women: Case Issues in Biblical Interpretation.* Scottdale, Pa.: Herald, 1983. 366 pp. A Mennonite New Testament scholar shows how the Bible has been used by Christians on opposing sides of four issues. A very illuminating analysis of the problems involved in the use of the Bible for social issues, with helpful suggestions.

Tambasco, Anthony J. "The Bible and Nuclear War: A Case Study in Methodology for Christian Biblical Ethics." *BTB* 13 (1983): 75-81. A Roman Catholic biblical scholar discusses the hermeneutics used by Dale Aukerman in *Darkening Valley* (see above).

Yoder, John Howard. *The Original Revolution: Essays on Christian Pacifism.* Scottdale, Pa.: Herald, 1977. In ch. 4, "If Abraham Is Our Father" (85-104), a Mennonite ethicist urges Christians to understand the warfare in the Hebrew Bible as the ancient Israelites would have—as a limitation of militarism and nationalism. See also Yoder, *The Politics of Jesus* (Grand Rapids: Wm. B. Eerdmans, 1972), especially ch. 4, "God Will Fight for Us" (78-89); and " 'To Your Tents, O Israel': The Legacy of Israel's Experience with Holy War." *Studies in Religion/Sciences religieuses* 18 (1989): 345-362. To "stand fast" means, negatively, only to refrain from coercion and, positively, to celebrate the inseparability of God's power and love.

See also many of the works in Section I above.

Princeton, New Jersey
6 August 1990:
45 years after Hiroshima

Printed in the United States
92648LV00006B/76/A

9 780802 805287